Bon Appétit
Every-Night Cooking

BON APPÉTIT
Every-Night Cooking

from the Editors of Bon Appétit

Condé Nast Books • Clarkson Potter/Publishers

New York

Broiled Herbed Polenta with Wild Mushrooms, page 101

For *Bon Appétit* Magazine
Barbara Fairchild, Editor-in-Chief
Laurie Glenn Buckle, Editor, Bon Appétit Books
Marcy MacDonald, Editorial Business Manager
Carri Marks, Editorial Production Director
Lynne Hartung, Editorial Production Manager
Sybil Shimazu Neubauer, Editorial Administrator
Laura Samuel Meyn, Assistant Editor
Marcia Hartmann Lewis, Editorial Support
Jeanne Thiel Kelley, Text and Food Research
Sarah Belk King, Supplemental Text
H. Abigail Bok, Copy Editor
Gaylen Ducker Grody, Research
Elizabeth A. Matlin, Index

For Condé Nast Books
Lisa Faith Phillips, Vice President and General Manager
Tom Downing, Direct Marketing Director
Deborah Williams, Operations Director
Jennifer Zalewski, Direct Marketing Associate
Barbara Giordano, Direct Marketing Associate
Eric Levy, Inventory Associate

Design: Ph.D
Photography: Leo Gong
Printed in association with Patrick Filley Associates, Inc.

Front Jacket: Spaghettini with Shrimp, Tomatoes and Garlic, page 42

Published by Clarkson Potter/Publishers, 299 Park Avenue, New York, New York 10171.
Member of the Crown Publishing Group. Random House, Inc. New York, Toronto, London, Sydney, Auckland

CLARKSON N. POTTER, POTTER, and colophon are trademarks of Random House, Inc.

Manufactured in Hong Kong

Library of Congress Cataloging-in-Publication Data is available upon request.

ISBN 0-609-60921-1

10 9 8 7 6 5 4 3 2 1

FIRST EDITION

Condé Nast Web Address: bonappetit.com
Random House Web Address: randomhouse.com
Bon Appétit Books Web Address: bonappetitbooks.com

Contents

Introduction

Unlike a board game, cooking every night doesn't come with instructions. How is it, exactly, that you are supposed to get from home to job to picking up the kids to home to getting dinner on in the wrinkle of a nose? Sometimes, just contemplating dinner is enough to send you home via a take-out window.

But what if there were a book that was part instruction, part inspiration and part just plain great food? What if cooking every night *were* more of a game and less of a chore? A game is fun. A game involves strategy and planning. It could work; and that's the thinking behind this book   your everyday guide to every-night cooking, complete with everything you need to know (from stocking the pantry to planning menus) and everything you want to eat (from quick-to-make pastas to supper-in-a-bowl soups to meatless main courses).

So call it a game, enlist the rest of your family as players, and plan a week's worth of moves. Everybody wins, and the prize is one delicious dinner after another.

Clockwise from top left: Summer Garden Soup, page 61; Turkey Cheeseburgers, page 71; Peanut Butter and Chocolate Chip Cookies, page 181; Lamb Kebabs with Peanut Sauce, page 151.

The Survival Guide

Were there rules to the game of cooking every night, they might look something like the information included in this section of the book. This is where we walk you through the how-tos of every-night cooking, beginning with stocking the pantry. Dinner's doomed when the cupboard is bare, so we offer step-by-step guidance to shopping for staples *and* storing them.

Then there's the equipment in your kitchen—do you have everything you need? Sometimes the right tool or pot or knife can make the difference between a time-consuming chore and a quick task. That advice is followed by more on menu planning, key to any successful every night cooking strategy. If you know on Sunday what you'll be cooking later in the week, then you've simplified the grocery shopping and answered the "what's for dinner?" question even before it's asked.

Shortcuts to cleanup, timesaving hints, grilling tips and advice on feeding the finicky (i.e., kids) round out this indispensable section, your best guide to the game.

Stocking the Pantry

How well are your pantry, refrigerator and freezer stocked? Keeping essential ingredients on hand means there's *always* something for dinner—and you won't have to stop at the grocery store after work. Use this list to stock your pantry according to your family's preferences.

PANTRY
olive oil
vegetable oil
granulated sugar
brown sugar
flour
cornstarch
arborio rice
long-grain rice
spaghetti, linguine,
   fettuccine
farfalle, penne, rotini,
   macaroni
couscous
cornmeal
barley
grits
dried black beans and
   white beans
dried lentils
dried wild mushrooms
breadcrumbs
raisins, dried cherries,
   dried apricots
oatmeal
potatoes
onions
garlic
shallots

CANNED GOODS
black, refried, garbanzo,
   pinto, kidney and
   canellini beans
whole, chopped and
   crushed tomatoes
tomato sauce, tomato
   paste
chicken, beef,
   vegetable and
   mushroom broths
coconut milk
green and *chipotle*
   chilies
salsa verde
tuna
anchovies
canned soups
pumpkin puree
pineapple chunks
   or rings

BOTTLED GOODS
black and green olives
olive paste
capers
marinated artichoke
   hearts
oil-packed sun-dried
   tomatoes
ketchup
mayonnaise
Dijon mustard
soy sauce
toasted sesame oil
chutney
hoisin sauce
barbecue sauce
pickles
red wine, Sherry, rice
   and balsamic
   vinegars
Worcestershire sauce
red and white wines
Sherry
Cognac or brandy
peanut butter
jams and jellies
salsas and hot sauces
molasses
honey
vanilla extract
almond extract

**DRIED HERBS AND
   SPICES**
allspice
bay leaves
cardamom
cayenne pepper
chili powder
cinnamon
cloves
coriander
cumin
curry powder
fennel seeds
ginger
herbes de Provence
nutmeg
oregano
paprika
sage
thyme

REFRIGERATOR
butter
eggs
milk
whipping cream
sour cream
yogurt
cream cheese
pesto
Parmesan cheese
cheddar and other
   cheeses
fresh ginger
lemons
tofu
carrots
celery

FREEZER
chicken breasts
   or thighs
ground beef
corn
peas
spinach
berries
ravioli or tortellini
smoked sausages
ice cream
sorbet
juice concentrates
fresh lemon juice
bacon
bread
frozen bread dough
tortillas
frozen pie crusts
wonton wrappers
pine nuts
walnuts

Shopping Tips

Once your kitchen is fully stocked, shopping is much less of a chore. Let the availability of fresh ingredients inspire you—buy produce that looks good, a special cut of meat or a kind of cheese that is on sale—and choose recipes based on those foods. Keep track of any essential ingredients (see "Stocking the Pantry") that you've used up, and restock regularly.

Another way to make shopping more fun is to explore different kinds of stores. It's boring going to the same supermarket every week with the same list—so branch out.

• **WAREHOUSE STORES** are terrific for families, and for anyone with ample storage space. Shoppers save money by buying quality products in bulk. Of course, even the best deal isn't worth it if you're not able to use the product up before it expires, so search for items that are shelf stable or ones that your family uses often. Some shoppers even join forces with friends and split the goods, benefiting from the savings without the hassle of finding storage for the surplus. The following items are usually good values at warehouse stores.

fresh cuts of meat and poultry	cleaning supplies
refrigerated and frozen entrées	paper towels, napkins
	granola bars, snacks
	individual juice drinks
sandwich meats	cereal
sandwich breads	soups
fruits, vegetables	soda
cheeses	wine, beer
vegetable oil, olive oil	coffee
mustard, ketchup, mayonnaise	spirits

• **ON-LINE GROCERY SHOPPING,** though not as thrifty as searching out the sale items in a traditional grocery store, is a great timesaver.

(continued on page 12)

Storage

After you've stocked up on ingredients, be sure to store them properly so they'll last as long as possible. Your pantry might be as small as a kitchen cabinet or as large as a walk-in closet; whatever your space, make sure it's cool and dry. Avoid storing foods near the oven or dishwasher, where heat can shorten their shelf life. Check "use by" dates on everything from canned goods to meats and poultry before consuming. To prevent freezer burn, wrap items in plastic wrap and foil, then enclose in freezer bags before freezing. Make sure your refrigerator is cold enough—about 37°F—to keep food from spoiling. Follow these storage guidelines.

flours and grains: airtight container in pantry	fruit: cool, dry place
cookies and crackers: airtight container in pantry	dairy: coldest part of refrigerator
	fresh herbs: in glass of water in refrigerator
oils: pantry or refrigerator	meats and chicken: refrigerator or freezer
butter: refrigerator or freezer	
potatoes: pantry or refrigerator	dried fruits: refrigerator or pantry
onions and garlic: pantry	nuts: freezer
vegetables: crisper drawer in refrigerator	breads: pantry or freezer

Customers select groceries on-line in a matter of minutes, then pay with a credit card and set up a delivery time. Some of the better sites, like peapod.com and homegrocer.com, prompt shoppers through the steps, including searching for favorite brand-name items and adding them to a virtual shopping cart. These or similar services are available in most major metropolitan areas in the United States, and they are expected to branch out quickly over the next couple of years or so.

• **FARMERS' MARKETS** are among the most satisfying places to shop. Not only are your purchases a great way to support local farmers, but you and your family will enjoy the freshest in-season produce available; in fact, the produce will probably last longer than what you would buy in a store. Many farmers' markets also feature freshly baked breads, cut flowers for the table and food stands with local specialties like tamales, apple butter and handmade cheeses.

• **SPECIALTY STORES** can be anything from small ethnic grocery stores to upscale food markets. Ethnic grocery stores are great sources for ingredients specific to that cuisine. A small container of pine nuts, for instance, is fairly expensive in a supermarket, but a Middle Eastern grocer would sell them in larger quantities for less. Upscale food markets often have great full-service delis that make putting dinner on the table even easier. They also carry imported foods that may not be available at your regular supermarket—such as high-quality European baking chocolate or top-notch extra-virgin olive oil from Tuscany.

Budgeting How-tos

The best way to save on your grocery bill is to be flexible. Take a look at supermarket advertisements in the newspaper, and plan meals around what's on sale. Take advantage of any specials; for instance, if whole chickens go on sale, buy one to prepare and another to freeze for later. Stock up on the produce that's bargain-priced— chances are, it's in season too.

And purchase cereals, snacks and treats like ice cream only when they're on sale.

Supermarket clubs are a trend among many of the chains throughout the country. If your market has one of these, by all means participate. It often requires nothing more than attaching a tag to your key chain and reminding the checker to scan it; the often-significant savings are usually itemized on your receipt.

Coupons are another way to save; the trick is to cut coupons only for items you use, then remember to take them to the market with you. Some stores will double the value of your coupon, so if you are a coupon clipper, be sure to shop where you'll get the most for your efforts.

Essential Equipment

The flip side to having a well-stocked cupboard is having a complete set of equipment. And while having pasta, cream and cheese on hand can turn dinner into something special, having something to grate the cheese with and drain the pasta in is essential. Using the right equipment also saves you time and frustration. Small appliances like handheld electric mixers and food processors will speed you through otherwise laborious recipes. Good-quality pots, pans and knives, in particular, are worth the investment for their long lives and performance. Take a survey of your kitchen and then set out to make sure it's outfitted with the following items.

a powerful blender: immersion, countertop or both

food processor with grating, slicing and chopping attachments

handheld electric mixer

heavy-duty stand mixer

microwave oven

stainless steel or anodized aluminum saucepans:
   various sizes, including 1-quart and 2-quart capacities

stainless steel skillets with lids:
   various sizes, including an 8- to 10-inch skillet

nonstick skillets in various sizes

large ovenproof covered casserole dish (also known as a Dutch oven)

metal or glass mixing bowls in various sizes

mesh colanders in a few sizes

rubber and metal spatulas

large slotted spoon

large ladle

several wooden spoons

measuring cups in all sizes, including an 8-cup-capacity measuring cup
   (doubles as a mixing bowl), $2/3$- and $3/4$-cup measures

a few sets of deep measuring spoons

whisks: small, medium and large

steamer basket

two large wooden cutting boards, one for meats and one for produce

heavy, sharp knives, including large chef's knife; long, sharp slicer;
   serrated bread knife; several paring knives

Menu Planning

When it comes to planning dinner, think *main course, side dish, vegetable and dessert.* The main dish is usually rich in protein—meat, eggs, cheese, tofu, beans or pasta. For a side dish, choose a starch like rice, barley, couscous, potatoes or bread. Vegetables are so healthy you may want to serve more than one. If you do, pair a green vegetable with another type—green beans with carrots, for example, or broccoli with cauliflower. It also adds interest to a menu to pair a cooked vegetable with a raw one—try sautéed zucchini with sliced tomatoes or a mixed green salad with grilled eggplant. Dessert can be as simple as a scoop of ice cream or sorbet, a piece of fresh fruit or a cookie from the bakery.

When planning a menu, be sure to keep variety in mind. Consider the color, texture and flavor of each dish, and avoid repeating elements. If you shop for the entire week in one trip, be sure to serve the most perishable items, such as fish or delicate vegetables, first. As an alternative to planning full menus, "one-dish" meals can serve as the main course and vegetable combined; spinach lasagna, for example, requires only crusty bread and a glass of wine to make it a meal.

These menus can be used as a guide. Develop your own combinations as you discover recipes you like and want to make again, in keeping with what's in season, or in accordance with how much time you have or what you have on hand.

S Sage-roasted Turkey with Caramelized Onions (page 168)
Steamed Brussels Sprouts
Mashed Sweet Potatoes
Corn Bread
Pear Cake with Pecan Praline Topping (page 201)

M Ravioli with Sage Cream Sauce (page 41)
Mixed Baby Greens with Balsamic Vinaigrette
Crusty Italian Bread
Biscotti
Coffee or Hot Chocolate

T Tortilla Chips with Purchased Guacamole and Salsa
Turkey Enchiladas (page 169)
Black Beans
Rice
Rainbow Sherbet

W Grilled T-Bone Steaks Florentine (page 128)
Slender Green Beans with Toasted Pine Nuts
Baked Potatoes
Cheesecake from the Market

T Arugula and Bacon Quiche (page 24)
Roasted Asparagus
Steamed Red-skinned New Potatoes
Madeleines from the Bakery

F Lemon and Tarragon Baked Chicken (page 147)
Sautéed Broccoli
Glazed Carrots
Angel Food Cake with Fresh Strawberries

S Rosemary-roasted Salmon (page 198)
Sautéed Swiss Chard
Couscous
Brownie Sundaes (make the brownies from a mix)

S Roasted Pork Loin with Garlic and Rosemary (page 164)
Mashed Yukon Gold Potatoes
Peas with Butter and Grated Parmesan Cheese
Apple Pie from the Bakery

M Tuscan Pork and Rice Salad (page 165)
Focaccia Bread
Fresh Seasonal Fruit

T Teriyaki Chicken and Noodles (page 33)
Sautéed Snow Peas
Fortune Cookies
Green Tea

W Peas and Potatoes Masala (page 104)
Steamed Basmati Rice
Purchased *Naan* or Pita Bread
Vanilla Frozen Yogurt with Chopped Fresh Mango

T Garlic-Pancetta Pizzas (page 97)
Spinach Salad
Raspberry Sorbet

F Baked Potatoes with Spiced Beef Chili (page 85)
Tossed Green Salad with Ranch Dressing
Steamed Corn on the Cob
Carrot Cake from the Bakery

S Parsley, Sage, Rosemary and Thyme
Chicken (page 161)
Roasted Potatoes and Shallots
Sautéed Broccoli Florets
Lemon Cream Tartlets (page 189)

Kidssentials

If you have kids, you already know how hard it can be to make a dinner both you and they will like, and to get them fed before they crumble from hunger. Sometimes you manage a meal that comes in on time and satisfies everybody, sometimes you don't. For those nights when time is limited, keep the kitchen stocked with favored foods that can quickly become dinner.

MAIN COURSES

pasta, marinara sauce and grated Parmesan cheese

hot dogs or turkey dogs (tofu dogs for vegetarians) and hot dog buns

flour tortillas and grated Monterey Jack cheese for quesadillas

ground hamburger or turkey and hamburger buns

bread, canned tuna and sliced cheese for tuna melts

bread and sliced cheese for grilled cheese sandwiches

rice, eggs and assorted vegetables for stir-fried rice

purchased pizza crusts (or English muffins or pita bread), marinara sauce, cheese and other toppings

potatoes and toppings for baked-potato suppers

bread and eggs for scrambled eggs on toast

tortillas or lavash and sliced deli meats for wraps

LUNCHES AND SNACKS

carrot sticks or baby carrots

peas in the pod

cherry tomatoes

celery

salad mixes in bags

a variety of fresh fruits

rice and couscous

assorted breads (including bagels)

crackers and breadsticks

rice cakes

string cheese in single-serving packages

pretzels

popcorn

raisins

Cleanup Shortcuts

Everyone's least favorite part of cooking is undoubtedly cleaning up. But there *are* steps you can take to make it a little easier. Try the following.

• Line roasting pans with aluminum foil before roasting meats.
• Use parchment paper or Silpats to line baking sheets.
• Prepare dinner in one skillet when possible.
• Clean up as you cook; wash cookware and utensils while dinner is in the oven or on the stove.
• Fill pots and pans with soapy water to soak during dinner, making them easier to clean later.
• Solicit help clearing the table, rinsing dishes and loading the dishwasher.

Grilling 101

Grilling is fast and easy and requires less cleanup than cooking on the stove or in the oven (no pots and pans to contend with)—all of which makes it ideal for every-night cooking. Add to that the pleasure of getting outside for a bit at the end of the day (even if it's chilly—just toss on a jacket and grab your tongs), and it's easy to see why grilling is as popular as it is.

In the pages that follow, you'll find a number of recipes for grilled main courses. You don't always need a recipe, though, as the smoke and fire add their own delicious flavor.

EXPERIMENT WITH ANY OF THESE ON THE GRILL:	KEEP THESE THINGS ON HAND:
chicken breasts	long-handled spatula and tongs
steaks	heavy-duty oven mitts
pork chops	charcoal and lighter fluid or a butane tank
sausages and bell peppers	(preferably two)
kebabs: meat, seafood, chicken or tofu	metal and/or bamboo skewers
vegetables: portobello mushrooms, eggplant and	wood chips
zucchini, especially	instant-read thermometerr

Timesaving Techniques

How can you turn out home-cooked meals quickly? Try borrowing the concept of *mis en place* (everything put in place) from professional chefs. This tried-and-true method consists of preparing, measuring and setting aside every ingredient for the dish you're cooking   before you start. (Picture your favorite cooking show.) This method of organization will save you the errors, stress and mess that can result from hasty measuring. In fact, you'll find it allows you to assemble and cook each dish in no time. Here are some other ideas to consider.

- Read through the recipe before you begin.
- Prepare ingredients that won't discolor—like onions, carrots and celery—hours ahead, if you like.
- Prepare more food than you need; leftovers can be served again for an easy dinner or packed for lunch.
- If you cook with certain items often, have them ready. For instance, if you cook with pureed chipotle chilies, puree them and keep them chilled. If you cook with fresh lemon juice, freeze it in ice cube trays.
- Plant an herb garden so you always have the herbs you need at your fingertips.

Dinner Plans

Because what to cook for dinner can depend on any number of circumstances and conditions, from the weather to what you have (or don't have) on hand, from who's around the table to how much time you have (or don't have) to cook, it's often easier to think in terms of kind of dish or type of meal. Some nights are just made for a warming bowl of soup or a cooling main-course salad; other nights you need a supper the children are sure to like (turn to "Kid Fare, Plus," page 150) or the quickest dinner going (see "Pizzas Better Than Delivered," page 90).

That's why this section of the book is organized by "kind": kind of meal ("Breakfast for Dinner," page 20), kind of technique ("Instant Stir-fries," page 30) or kind of food ("Baked Potatoes and Beyond," page 80). Within this framework, you can add your own parameters, from family preferences to seasonal availability. The recipes are often made even more flexible with suggested variations. In addition, there are menu suggestions (easy, no-extra-work ideas for side dishes) and do-ahead tips.

Breakfast for Dinner

Sometimes the best dinner really is breakfast—or breakfast foods. Familiar morning fare can make a satisfying supper, one that tastes as good at the end of the day as it would at the beginning.

Buttermilk Pancakes
with Blueberry Compote

This classic recipe makes a complete dinner when served with bacon and hash browns. Keep cooked pancakes warm in a 200°F oven while making enough for everyone.

VARIATION: Try frozen raspberries instead of blueberries in the compote.
DO-AHEAD: Pre-measure and mix the dry ingredients to cut preparation time. Make compote.

MAKES ABOUT 18

2½ cups all purpose flour

¼ cup sugar

2 teaspoons baking powder

2 teaspoons baking soda

1 teaspoon salt

2 cups buttermilk

2 cups sour cream

2 large eggs

4 teaspoons vanilla extract

3 tablespoons unsalted butter

Additional unsalted butter

Blueberry Compote (see recipe)

Whisk first 5 ingredients in large bowl. Whisk buttermilk, sour cream, eggs and vanilla in another large bowl. Add to dry ingredients. Stir until batter is just blended but still lumpy (do not overmix).

Melt ½ tablespoon butter on griddle over medium heat. Pour batter by ¼ cupfuls onto griddle, spacing 2 inches apart. Cook until bubbles break on surface, about 3 minutes. Turn pancakes over. Cook until bottoms are golden, 3 minutes. Transfer to plates. Repeat with remaining batter, adding butter to skillet as needed. Serve immediately with butter and Blueberry Compote.

Blueberry Compote

2½ cups frozen blueberries, unthawed

⅓ cup sugar

⅓ cup water

MAKES ABOUT
1½ CUPS

Combine 1½ cups blueberries, sugar and ⅓ cup water in heavy small saucepan. Simmer over medium heat until berries burst, stirring often, about 10 minutes. Add remaining 1 cup berries. Cook until compote coats spoon, stirring often, about 8 minutes. *(Can be made 3 days ahead. Cool compote, then cover and refrigerate. Rewarm before serving.)* Serve warm.

Baked French Toast
with Cardamom and Marmalade

Have sausage patties and fresh fruit on the side to round out the menu.

VARIATION: This would be delicious made with apricot or seedless raspberry jam in place of the orange marmalade. On a busy night, serve with maple syrup instead of the homemade citrus syrup to cut preparation time. Kids may prefer less cardamom—or none.

DO-AHEAD: Note that this can be prepared in the morning; just pop it in the oven after work and put together the side dishes while it bakes.

10 SERVINGS

FRENCH TOAST

1¼ cups orange marmalade

10 4x4x1-inch slices egg bread

1¼ cups whole milk

¾ cup whipping cream

½ cup sugar

3 large egg yolks

3 large eggs

1¼ teaspoons ground cardamom

1 teaspoon grated orange peel

1 teaspoon grated lemon peel

CITRUS SYRUP

1¼ cups light corn syrup

3 tablespoons fresh lemon juice

2 tablespoons grated orange peel

4 teaspoons sugar

1 tablespoon grated lemon peel

Powdered sugar

FOR FRENCH TOAST: Butter 15x10x2-inch glass baking dish. Spread marmalade evenly over 1 side of each bread slice. Cut slices diagonally in half, forming triangles. Arrange triangles crosswise in dish, marmalade side up, overlapping slightly.

Whisk milk and next 7 ingredients in large bowl. Pour custard over bread. Let bread stand 1 hour, basting occasionally, or cover and refrigerate up to 8 hours.

FOR CITRUS SYRUP: Mix first 5 ingredients in small bowl, stirring until sugar dissolves. Let stand at least 1 hour. *(Can be made 3 days ahead. Cover with plastic and refrigerate.)*

Preheat oven to 350°F. Bake French toast, uncovered, until puffed and golden brown, approximately 50 minutes. Sprinkle with powdered sugar; serve with citrus syrup.

Huevos Rancheros

The traditional Mexican egg dish is made simple here with purchased salsa. Serve with sliced oranges and jicama sticks.

VARIATION: Look for sun-dried-tomato- or jalapeño-flavored tortillas to make this dish different. Choose mild, medium or hot salsa to suit your taste. Try the recipe with regular Monterey Jack or Colby Jack instead of the hot pepper variety if you prefer less heat.
DO-AHEAD: Prepare the sauce a day ahead. The tortillas can be kept warm in the oven until needed. Just before serving, bring the sauce to a simmer and cook the eggs.

¾ cup bottled salsa

1 medium plum tomato, chopped

3 tablespoons chopped fresh cilantro

4 tablespoons vegetable oil

4 7- to 9-inch flour or corn tortillas, flavored or plain

8 large eggs

1½ cups (packed) grated hot pepper Monterey Jack cheese (about 6 ounces)

4 SERVINGS

Preheat oven to 350°F. Mix first 3 ingredients in medium saucepan; set sauce aside. Heat 2 tablespoons oil in heavy large skillet over medium-high heat. Add 1 tortilla and cook until just beginning to brown, about 30 seconds. Using tongs, turn tortilla over and heat 10 seconds. Transfer to large sheet of foil. Repeat with remaining tortillas. Enclose tortillas in foil and place in oven to keep warm.

Divide remaining 2 tablespoons oil between 2 medium skillets and heat over medium heat. Break 4 eggs into each skillet; sprinkle with salt and pepper. Cook until just set on bottom, about 2 minutes. Sprinkle with grated cheese. Cover skillets; cook until eggs are cooked as desired and cheese melts, about 2 minutes. Meanwhile, bring sauce to boil over high heat.

Divide tortillas among 4 plates. Top each with 2 eggs, then warm sauce.

Arugula and Bacon Quiche

Quiche is back—and for good reason: It makes a terrific weeknight meal because it can be served warm, at room temperature or even cold, and with a purchased pie crust on hand, it's easy to throw together. A green salad with a balsamic and olive oil vinaigrette is all that's needed to go with this simple but sophisticated entrée.

VARIATION: Try spinach, prosciutto and Swiss cheese instead of arugula, bacon and Gruyère.
DO-AHEAD: Cover and refrigerate any leftovers up to two days; a cold wedge of quiche makes a great lunch at your desk.

6 SERVINGS

1 purchased frozen 9-inch deep-dish pie crust

6 bacon slices, cut into ½-inch pieces

½ cup chopped shallots

8 ounces arugula, stems trimmed, leaves coarsely chopped (about 5½ cups)

2 teaspoons balsamic vinegar

1 cup whipping cream

3 large eggs

½ teaspoon salt

¼ teaspoon ground black pepper

¾ cup shredded Gruyère cheese (about 2½ ounces)

Preheat oven to 400°F. Thaw pie crust 10 minutes. Bake crust until pale golden, about 12 minutes. Transfer to rack and cool. Reduce oven temperature to 375°F.

Cook bacon in heavy medium skillet over medium-high heat until crisp, about 5 minutes. Using slotted spoon, transfer to paper towels and drain. Add shallots to same skillet and sauté until tender, about 2 minutes. Add arugula and sauté until just wilted, about 1 minute. Remove from heat. Add balsamic vinegar; toss arugula to combine.

Sprinkle arugula mixture, then bacon over crust. Whisk cream, eggs, salt and pepper in large bowl to blend. Stir in cheese. Pour mixture into crust.

Bake quiche until filling is slightly puffed and golden, about 35 minutes. Let quiche stand for at least 10 minutes. Cut into wedges and serve warm or at room temperature.

Wild Mushroom, Shallot and Gruyère Omelets

Omelets make a simple supper; round out the menu with bread and baby greens.

VARIATION: These omelets would be delicious with a number of different fillings; try some of the following combinations in place of the mushrooms, shallots and Gruyère: asparagus and Fontina; avocado and pepper Jack cheese; smoked salmon, arugula and sour cream; sautéed bell peppers and white cheddar; crab, green onions and cilantro; canned green chilies, Jack cheese and red onions; or feta with spinach and dill.

DO-AHEAD: Prepare the filling in the morning.

---

4 tablespoons (½ stick) butter

4 ounces fresh wild mushrooms (such as shiitake or oyster), trimmed, sliced

2 large shallots, minced

1 tablespoon minced fresh parsley

6 large eggs

4 teaspoons cold water

⅔ cup grated Gruyère cheese (about 2 ounces)

Additional minced fresh parsley (optional)

2 SERVINGS

Melt 1 tablespoon butter in heavy small skillet over medium heat. Add mushrooms and shallots and sauté until mushrooms are tender, about 2 minutes. Season with salt and pepper. Remove from heat and mix in 1 tablespoon parsley. *(Can be prepared up to 8 hours ahead. Cover and refrigerate.)*

Beat 3 eggs and 2 teaspoons water in small bowl. Season with salt and pepper. Melt 1¼ tablespoons butter in small omelet pan over medium-high heat. Add egg mixture. Cook until almost set, tilting skillet and lifting egg mixture with spatula to allow uncooked portion to run underneath. Spoon half of cheese, then half of mushroom mixture down center of omelet. Fold omelet over filling in thirds and transfer to plate. Make second omelet with remaining eggs, water, salt, pepper, 1½ tablespoons butter, mushrooms and cheese. Garnish with additional parsley, if desired.

Asparagus and Egg Gratin with Fontina

For this easy one-dish meal, eggs are baked in wells made in a flavorful vegetable mixture in a gratin pan. Fruit would be a refreshing follow-up.

VARIATION: Ham would work in place of the Canadian bacon.

1 tablespoon butter

1 onion, chopped

8 ounces asparagus, cut on diagonal
   into 1-inch pieces

6 ounces unsliced Canadian bacon,
   cut into ½-inch cubes

⅓ cup plus 4 teaspoons whipping cream

Pinch of cayenne pepper

1 tablespoon Dijon mustard

4 large eggs
   Additional cayenne pepper

4 ounces Fontina cmeese, grated

Preheat oven to 375°F. Butter 9½-inch oval gratin pan. Melt 1 tablespoon butter in heavy medium skillet over medium heat. Add onion and cook until beginning to soften, about 5 minutes. Add asparagus; season with salt and pepper. Cook until asparagus begins to soften, about 4 minutes. Add bacon and stir 1 minute. Add ⅓ cup cream and pinch of cayenne pepper. Stir until heated through, about 1 minute. Mix in mustard. Transfer to prepared pan.

Make 4 wells in mixture, spacing evenly apart. Break 1 egg into each well. Drizzle 1 teaspoon cream over each egg. Sprinkle with salt, pepper and additional cayenne. Bake gratin until egg whites are beginning to set but are still runny, about 12 minutes.

Preheat broiler. Sprinkle cheese over dish. Broil gratin until cheese is melted and beginning to brown, about 30 seconds. Serve gratin immediately.

Confetti Scrambled Eggs

Any combination of bell peppers will work in this dish; buy what looks best at the market.

VARIATION: For a change, try chopping four to six slices of bacon in place of the pepperoni. Cook the bacon with the onions, pouring off most of the excess fat before adding the peppers.

DO-AHEAD: To save time later, chop the onions and peppers ahead, cover and refrigerate.   6 SERVINGS

¼ cup (½ stick) butter

2 cups chopped onions

1 4-ounce piece pepperoni sausage, chopped
(about 1 cup)

½ cup chopped red bell pepper

½ cup chopped yellow bell pepper

½ cup chopped green bell pepper

1 teaspoon dried marjoram

12 large eggs, beaten to blend

Melt butter in large nonstick skillet over low heat. Add chopped onions and sauté until very tender, about 8 minutes. Add pepperoni, all bell peppers and marjoram. Cook over low heat until bell peppers are crisp-tender, stirring occasionally, about 10 minutes. Pour in eggs. Stir over medium-low heat until eggs are just set, about 5 minutes. Transfer to bowl and serve.

THE BREAKFAST PANTRY

Eggs, potatoes, onions and bread. They're always available, always affordable. And they're probably in your kitchen—in some form or another—all the time. The simple, comforting foods that we usually associate with the morning meal can also become a satisfying supper—fast. Keep these things on hand.

- Eggs: For best flavor, buy them at a farmers' market.
- Potatoes: Russet and Idaho potatoes are best for baking and mashing. For making hash browns or home fries, use russet potatoes. Red-skinned new potatoes, which can be boiled or roasted, save prep time since you don't have to peel them.
- Bread: Just about any type of good-quality bread will make fine French toast; experiment with cinnamon, raisin and sourdough.
- Cheese: Cheddar, Parmesan, Gruyère and Monterey Jack marry well with most egg dishes.
- Breakfast Meats: Bacon, ham and sausage all make good accompaniments to breakfast-style dishes.
- Onions, Shallots and Green Onions: Whether you're adding them to eggs or potatoes, these can bring a dish to life.
- Frozen and Dried Fruits: Thawed drained berries can be added to pancake and waffle batter; they can also be included in a compote or sauce to serve atop breakfast foods. Dried fruits can be mixed into the batter for muffins and coffee cakes.

Potato and Green Onion Frittata

A frittata, Italy's version of the omelet, isn't filled or folded—instead, the ingredients are mixed in with the eggs, which are cooked on the stove, then broiled. Serve with an antipasti platter (made from purchased ingredients) for a simple dinner with Italian flair.

VARIATION: Frittatas can be as versatile as omelets; try adding chopped prosciutto, ham or cooked crumbled sausage for a heartier version of this dish.

DO-AHEAD: Unlike omelets, frittatas can be made ahead and refrigerated, then served cold or at room temperature, alone or in a sandwich.

---

4 TO 6 SERVINGS

6 tablespoons butter

1¼ pounds red-skinned new potatoes (4 medium), quartered lengthwise, thinly sliced crosswise

8 green onions, sliced

12 large eggs

Sour cream

Minced green onion tops

Caviar (optional)

Melt 2 tablespoons butter in heavy broilerproof 12-inch skillet over medium-high heat. Add potatoes and sprinkle generously with pepper. Cook until crusty and just tender, stirring frequently and reducing heat if necessary to prevent burning, 8 minutes. Add sliced onions; stir 2 minutes. Cool slightly.

Beat eggs lightly in large bowl to blend. Stir in potatoes. Sprinkle with salt. Wipe out skillet. Add 4 tablespoons butter to skillet and melt over medium heat. Add egg mixture. Lift up edges of egg mixture with spatula, tipping pan to allow raw egg to flow under until edge forms, about 1 minute; do not stir. Reduce heat to low. Cover skillet and cook until eggs are almost set, about 5 minutes.

Meanwhile, preheat broiler. Uncover skillet and broil frittata until eggs are set, watching carefully. Garnish with sour cream, onion tops and caviar, if desired, and serve.

Citrus-Pecan Waffles

Beaten egg whites give these waffles a light and airy texture, while chopped pecans add crunch. Serve with home fries and sliced mangoes.

VARIATION: Try using macadamia nuts instead of pecans for a tropical twist on this recipe.

½ cup orange juice

½ cup milk

2 large eggs, separated, room temperature

3 tablespoons butter, melted

2 teaspoons fresh lemon juice

2 teaspoons grated orange peel

1½ teaspoons grated lemon peel

1 cup all purpose flour

½ teaspoon baking powder

½ teaspoon baking soda

½ teaspoon salt

⅔ cup finely chopped pecans

Pinch of cream of tartar

3 tablespoons sugar

Additional butter

Maple syrup

Whisk orange juice, milk, egg yolks, butter, lemon juice and grated peels in large bowl to blend. Combine flour, baking powder, baking soda and salt in medium bowl. Mix dry ingredients into orange juice mixture. Stir in pecans. Beat egg whites and cream of tartar in another bowl to soft peaks. Add sugar and beat until whites are stiff but not dry.

Preheat waffle iron according to manufacturer's instructions. Gently fold ¼ of whites into batter to lighten, then fold in remaining whites. Working in batches, spoon some batter onto iron; spread with spatula. Cover and cook until waffles are golden brown and cooked through. Repeat with remaining batter. Serve with additional butter and maple syrup.

Instant Stir-fries

Their very simplicity—that's what's so great about stir-fries. That, and the fact that they taste great and are as good for you as they are to eat.

Scallop Stir-fry with Crispy Noodle Pancake

Complete the meal with fortune cookies and mixed fruit salad.

VARIATION: Shrimp can be used instead of scallops; rice can stand in for the pancake.

¾ cup canned low-salt chicken broth

2 tablespoons oyster sauce

1 tablespoon cornstarch

½ teaspoon oriental sesame oil

2½ tablespoons vegetable oil

2 small carrots, peeled, thinly sliced on diagonal

8 ounces mushrooms, thinly sliced

6 ounces snow peas, stringed

4 green onions, sliced

2 tablespoons minced peeled fresh ginger

½ pound sea scallops, halved crosswise

Crispy Noodle Pancake (see recipe)

Combine first 4 ingredients in small bowl. Heat 1½ tablespoons vegetable oil in wok or heavy large skillet over high heat. Add carrots and stir-fry 1 minute. Add mushrooms and stir-fry 1½ minutes. Add snow peas and stir-fry until bright green, about 1½ minutes. Transfer to bowl.

Heat remaining 1 tablespoon vegetable oil in same wok or skillet over high heat. Add onions and ginger and stir-fry until aromatic, about 30 seconds. Add scallops and stir-fry 1½ minutes. Stir broth mixture to dissolve cornstarch and add to wok. Stir until sauce thickens. Return vegetables to wok and stir until coated with sauce. Spoon over noodle pancake and serve.

Crispy Noodle Pancake

6 ounces fresh chow mein noodles

4 green onions, chopped

1 teaspoon plus 1½ tablespoons vegetable oil

1½ tablespoons oriental sesame oil

Cook noodles in large pot of boiling water 1½ minutes, stirring occasionally. Drain. Rinse with cold water. Drain well. Toss with green onions, 1 teaspoon vegetable oil and pepper in bowl.

Heat 1½ tablespoons vegetable oil and sesame oil in heavy 9-inch nonstick skillet over medium heat. Add noodles and flatten slightly. Cook without stirring until light brown, about 6 minutes. Turn and cook second side until light brown, 6 minutes. Drain on paper towels. Cut into wedges.

Singapore Shrimp Stir-fry

Steam white rice to serve with this 15-minute stir-fry. Check the Asian foods section of your supermarket for the Thai oil and ginger soy sauce; you might find the unsweetened coconut milk and curry paste there too.

VARIATION: Chicken tenders would work in place of the shrimp in this dish.

¼ cup Thai oil or other flavored cooking oil

1¼ pounds uncooked medium shrimp, peeled, deveined

1 16-ounce package mixed stir-fry vegetables (thawed, if frozen; including snow peas, carrots, onion and celery)

1⅓ cups canned unsweetened coconut milk*

¼ cup ginger-flavored or spicy soy sauce

2 teaspoons Thai red or green curry paste*

Chopped green onions

Heat oil in heavy large skillet or wok over high heat. Add shrimp and stir-fry until just cooked through, about 4 minutes. Using slotted spoon, transfer shrimp to plate. Add vegetables to skillet and stir-fry 4 minutes. Add coconut milk, soy sauce and curry paste. Boil until sauce is slightly thickened, stirring frequently, about 6 minutes. Return shrimp and any accumulated juices to skillet. Stir 30 seconds; season with salt and pepper. Transfer to bowl; sprinkle with green onions.

*Coconut milk is available at Indian, Southeast Asian and Latin American markets and many supermarkets. Look for curry paste at Asian markets and in the Asian foods section of many supermarkets.

Teriyaki Chicken and Noodles

Serve with a salad of snow peas and sliced radishes in a ginger vinaigrette.

VARIATION: Turkey breast would work well in place of the chicken breast here.

4 SERVINGS

1 pound dried oriental noodles (such as soba
  or udon) or linguine, broken in half

2 tablespoons oriental sesame oil

¼ cup vegetable oil

4 skinless boneless chicken breast halves,
  cut crosswise into ⅓-inch-thick strips

1 bunch green onions, sliced on diagonal
  into 1-inch pieces

2 carrots, peeled, very thinly sliced on diagonal

½ teaspoon dried crushed red pepper

¾ cup purchased teriyaki sauce

Cook noodles in large pot of boiling salted water until just tender. Drain well; return to pot. Add sesame oil and toss to coat. Set noodles aside.

Heat vegetable oil in heavy large skillet over high heat. Sprinkle chicken with salt and pepper. Add chicken to skillet and sauté until no longer pink, about 3 minutes. Add green onions, carrots and dried red pepper. Stir-fry until vegetables are crisp-tender but still bright in color and chicken is cooked through, about 2 minutes longer. Add noodles and teriyaki sauce and toss to blend well. Serve immediately.

THE BUILDING BLOCKS OF A STIR-FRY

Stir-frying is fast. It's even faster if all of the ingredients are on hand. There are several parts to a stir-fried meal: the protein, the starch, the vegetables and the seasonings. The next time you shop, consider adding these "building blocks" of a stir-fry to your grocery list so that everything is ready when you are.

- Protein: Scallops, shrimp, pork tenderloin, flank steak and boneless chicken can be frozen and then thawed quickly. Firm water-packed tofu keeps one to two weeks.
- Starch: Try fragrant jasmine rice, short-grain Japanese "sticky" rice (it's easier to pick up with chopsticks) or brown rice. Many noodles—cellophane, *soba* and *ramen*—keep well in the pantry and cook in just minutes.
- Vegetables: Celery, bell peppers, carrots, green beans and green onions are always in season and work in virtually any stir-fry. Have frozen snow peas, *edamame*, spinach and peas on hand in the freezer, and canned water chestnuts, baby corn and bamboo shoots on the pantry shelf.
- Seasonings: Soy sauce, oyster sauce, Thai fish sauce, sesame oil, chili paste, teriyaki sauce, hoisin sauce, Thai red curry paste, rice vinegar and bean paste (miso) all make great additions to stir-fries. Don't forget a fresh touch, too—it might include chopped cilantro; grated orange, lemon or lime peel; or minced ginger.

Asian-Style Pork and Green Bean Stir-fry

Start with take-out sushi, then have this stir-fry with steamed rice or Asian noodles, such as *soba* or *ramen*. For color, add a cucumber and tomato salad sprinkled with rice vinegar.

VARIATION: Lean beef, such as eye of round, would be a good replacement for the pork.

DO-AHEAD: Note that the pork can marinate for up to four hours.

2 tablespoons soy sauce

2 tablespoons honey

1 tablespoon minced peeled fresh ginger

¼ teaspoon dried crushed red pepper

1 12-ounce pork tenderloin, fat trimmed, cut into ⅓-inch-thick strips

1 pound green beans, trimmed

1 tablespoon peanut oil

⅓ cup orange juice

1 teaspoon rice vinegar

1 teaspoon cornstarch

1 teaspoon grated orange peel

1 garlic clove, minced

Mix first 4 ingredients in 13x9x2-inch glass baking dish. Add pork tenderloin and toss to coat. Cover and let stand at room temperature 1 hour or refrigerate up to 4 hours.

Cook beans in large pot of boiling salted water until just crisp-tender. Drain.

Heat oil in large nonstick skillet over medium heat. Add pork, reserving marinade in dish. Sauté pork until almost cooked through, about 6 minutes. Add beans to skillet and sauté until beginning to brown and pork is cooked through, about 3 minutes.

Whisk orange juice, vinegar, cornstarch and reserved marinade in small bowl. Add orange peel, garlic and orange juice mixture to pork mixture in skillet. Stir until sauce boils, thickens slightly and coats bean-pork mixture, about 1 minute. Season with salt and pepper. Transfer to bowl and serve.

Beef, Mushroom and Broccoli Stir-fry

This popular Chinese menu classic is even better when made at home.

VARIATION: For a vegetarian entrée, use one 12-ounce package of firm or extra-firm tofu in place of the beef. Cut the tofu into ¾-inch cubes and marinate as if using beef. Pork or chicken would also work in this recipe.

---

1 pound flank steak

3 tablespoons water

7 tablespoons vegetable oil

4 tablespoons soy sauce

8 teaspoons cornstarch

6 tablespoons plus 1 cup canned low-salt chicken broth

¼ cup white wine

2 tablespoons oyster sauce

4 teaspoons oriental sesame oil

½ teaspoon sugar

6 quarter-size slices peeled fresh ginger, minced

2 pounds broccoli, cut into florets (stems discarded)

1 pound mushrooms, sliced

Steamed rice

4 SERVINGS

Cut steak with grain into 2-inch-wide pieces, then slice thinly across grain. Combine 3 tablespoons water, 2 tablespoons vegetable oil, 2 tablespoons soy sauce and 2 teaspoons cornstarch in large bowl. Add steak and stir to coat. Refrigerate at least 30 minutes.

Combine 6 tablespoons broth, remaining 2 tablespoons soy sauce, 6 teaspoons cornstarch, wine and next 3 ingredients in small bowl, stirring to dissolve cornstarch completely.

Heat 2 tablespoons vegetable oil in wok or heavy large skillet over high heat. Add steak with marinade and stir-fry until no longer pink, about 2 minutes. Transfer to platter. Add 2 tablespoons vegetable oil to wok. Add ginger and stir until aromatic, about 30 seconds. Add broccoli and stir-fry 1 minute. Add 1 cup broth. Cover, reduce heat and simmer 2½ minutes. Transfer broccoli to bowl. Add 1 tablespoon vegetable oil to wok. Add mushrooms; cook 2 minutes. Return steak and broccoli to wok. Stir sauce, add to wok and stir until sauce thickens, about 30 seconds. Transfer mixture to platter. Serve immediately with steamed rice.

Spicy Tofu and Vegetable Stir-fry with Soba Noodles

Chili-garlic paste, a bottled condiment available in the Asian foods section of most supermarkets, is a terrific ingredient to have on hand for its big flavor and spicy kick.

VARIATION: For those who don't like tofu, try this dish with sautéed shrimp or scallops.

2 TO 4 SERVINGS

1 ounce dried shiitake mushrooms

2 cups hot water

1 14-ounce package firm Chinese tofu

1 tablespoon plus 1 teaspoon cornstarch

2 teaspoons chili-garlic paste

2 tablespoons light soy sauce

8 ounces buckwheat soba noodles or linguine

2 tablespoons oriental sesame oil

2 tablespoons vegetable oil

1 bunch green onions, chopped

2 tablespoons minced peeled fresh ginger

6 large bok choy leaves, cut crosswise into ¼-inch-thick slices

5 ounces snow peas, trimmed

Place mushrooms in bowl. Cover with 2 cups hot water and let stand until softened, about 30 minutes. Drain tofu on paper towels 20 minutes. Cut tofu into ¾-inch pieces and drain on paper towels.

Drain mushrooms, reserving soaking liquid. Squeeze liquid from mushrooms, then slice, discarding stems. Pour 1 cup soaking liquid into small cup. Mix in cornstarch. Combine remaining soaking liquid, chili-garlic paste and soy sauce in another cup.

Cook soba in large pot of boiling salted water until tender but still firm to bite. Drain thoroughly. Toss noodles with 1 tablespoon sesame oil.

Meanwhile, heat vegetable oil in wok or heavy large skillet over high heat. Add chopped green onions and fresh ginger and stir until aromatic, about 30 seconds. Add bok choy and stir 2 minutes. Add mushrooms and snow peas and stir to coat with oil. Sprinkle with salt. Add chili paste mixture. Cover and boil until vegetables are just crisp-tender, about 1 minute. Uncover, add tofu and simmer until heated through. Stir cornstarch mixture to combine. Add to wok and stir gently until sauce thickens. Mix in remaining 1 tablespoon sesame oil.

Spoon vegetable mixture over soba noodles and serve immediately.

Stir-fried Rice with Eggs, Peas and Parmesan

This simple dish can be pulled together even when your cupboard is at its barest. It also makes good use of leftover rice. A salad of snow peas, bean sprouts and chopped peanuts with a rice vinegar dressing would round out the meal.

VARIATION: The combination of vegetables in this dish can vary according to what you have on hand: Frozen shelled *edamame* or lima beans can stand in for the peas, and green or yellow bell pepper would work in place of red bell pepper.

½ cup chopped carrots

3 large eggs

2 large egg whites

2 tablespoons freshly grated Parmesan cheese

1 tablespoon olive oil

½ cup chopped red onion

2 garlic cloves, minced

½ cup frozen petite peas, thawed

¼ cup finely chopped red bell pepper

2 cups cooked long-grain white rice
(about ¾ cup raw), room temperature

2 tablespoons thinly sliced fresh basil

2 tablespoons pine nuts, toasted

Cook carrots in small pot of boiling water until tender, about 5 minutes. Drain. In medium bowl, whisk eggs and egg whites until frothy. Add 1 tablespoon Parmesan and sprinkle with salt and pepper.

Heat oil in medium nonstick skillet over medium heat. Add onion and stir until almost tender, about 3 minutes. Add garlic and stir 1 minute longer. Add carrots, peas and red bell pepper. Stir until heated through, about 1 minute. Add rice and basil. Stir until heated through. Add egg mixture. Stir and fold until eggs are just set, about 2 minutes. Season with salt and pepper. Spoon onto platter. Sprinkle with pine nuts and remaining 1 tablespoon Parmesan cheese and serve.

Stir-fried Beef with Bell Peppers and Spicy Sauce

A well-stocked cupboard (complete with chili paste and bean paste) makes the most of this otherwise simple combination of ingredients.

VARIATION: Any lean beef would work here; try eye of round or top sirloin.
DO-AHEAD: The beef can marinate overnight and the vegetables can be chopped, sealed in plastic bags and refrigerated ahead, leaving only the stir-frying to do before dinner.

4 SERVINGS

1 tablespoon rice wine or dry Sherry	1 small green bell pepper, thinly sliced
1 tablespoon soy sauce	3 green onions, chopped
1 teaspoon oriental sesame oil	2½ teaspoons chili-garlic paste or chili-garlic sauce*
1 teaspoon minced garlic	1½ teaspoons bean paste*
8 ounces beef tenderloin	Steamed rice
3 teaspoons peanut oil	
1 small red bell pepper, thinly sliced	

Combine first 4 ingredients in medium bowl. Cut beef into ¼-inch-thick slices. Cut each slice into ¼-inch-wide strips. Add to bowl and toss. Let stand 1 hour or cover and chill overnight.

Heat 2 teaspoons peanut oil in wok or heavy large skillet over high heat. Add beef and stir 45 seconds. Transfer beef to bowl. Add remaining 1 teaspoon peanut oil to wok. Add bell peppers and stir 1 minute. Mix in chopped green onions, chili-garlic paste and bean paste and cook 20 seconds. Stir in beef and cook until heated through, about 30 seconds. Serve over rice.

*Available at Asian markets and in the Asian foods section of some supermarkets.

Stir-fried Pork with Cashews

Serve this 15-minute stir-fry with steamed brown rice.

VARIATION: Turkey can be used in place of the pork. Buy cashew pieces instead of whole cashews—they're less expensive and work just as well in this dish.

2 tablespoons peanut oil	½ cup roasted unsalted cashews
1 pound boneless pork loin, cut into ½-inch strips	1½ tablespoons brown sugar
2 tablespoons soy sauce	
1⅔ cups matchstick-size strips carrots	1 tablespoon cornstarch
1½ cups diced green bell peppers	3 tablespoons water

4 SERVINGS

Heat peanut oil in wok or heavy large skillet over high heat. Add pork and stir until lightly browned, about 2 to 3 minutes. Add soy sauce and stir 1 minute. Reduce heat to medium. Stir in carrots. Cover and cook until carrots are crisp-tender, about 3 minutes. Add bell peppers and cashews and stir until bell peppers are crisp-tender, about 3 to 4 minutes. Add brown sugar and stir until dissolved, about 1 minute. Push pork and vegetables to side of wok.

Dissolve cornstarch in 3 tablespoons water in small bowl and add to wok. Stir until sauce thickens and clears, about 1 minute. Mix pork and vegetables into sauce. Season with salt.

Quick Pastas

When there's no quick and easy answer to "What's for dinner?" there's always pasta, a favorite of most (kids, especially) and a pantry regular. Dress it up with some other cupboard staples and supper is solved—deliciously.

Ravioli with Sage Cream Sauce

Ripe pear slices wrapped in prosciutto make an elegant yet easy starter, if you're so minded. Toss chopped endive, radicchio, fennel and strips of roasted red pepper with an oil and vinegar dressing to serve with this pasta.

VARIATION: Cheese- or butternut-squash-filled ravioli would also work well with this sauce; pine nuts can be used instead of pecans.

---

1 8- to 9-ounce package refrigerated
   vegetable-filled ravioli

1½ tablespoons butter
  ¼ cup chopped pecans
  ⅓ cup finely chopped shallots

1½ tablespoons chopped fresh sage or
   1½ teaspoons crumbled dried sage
  ¾ cup dry white wine
  ⅔ cup whipping cream

Parmesan cheese shavings
Fresh sage leaves (optional)

Cook ravioli in large pot of boiling salted water until just tender, about 8 minutes. Drain well.

Meanwhile, melt butter in heavy medium skillet over medium heat. Add pecans and stir until slightly darker and fragrant, about 3 minutes. Using slotted spoon, transfer pecans to small bowl. Add shallots and sage to same skillet. Sauté until fragrant, about 30 seconds. Add wine and cream. Increase heat and boil until sauce is reduced to generous ¾ cup, about 5 minutes.

Add ravioli to sauce; toss. Season to taste with salt and pepper. Divide between large bowls. Sprinkle with pecans and Parmesan shavings. Garnish with fresh sage, if desired, and serve.

Spaghettini with Shrimp, Tomatoes and Garlic

Velveting—the Chinese technique of marinating chicken in egg white and cornstarch—is used with shrimp for tender, delicious results.

VARIATION: Rotelli or fusilli would work here in place of the spaghettini.

4 SERVINGS

2 tablespoons plus 1 cup dry white wine

2 large egg whites

3 teaspoons cornstarch

20 uncooked large shrimp, peeled, deveined

12 ounces spaghettini

3 tablespoons olive oil

3 cups diced plum tomatoes (about 20 ounces)

2 large garlic cloves, minced

¼ cup slivered fresh basil

Whisk 2 tablespoons wine, egg whites and cornstarch in large bowl to blend. Mix in shrimp; sprinkle generously with salt. Let shrimp stand for 10 minutes.

Meanwhile, cook pasta in large pot of boiling salted water until tender but still firm to bite.

Heat oil in heavy large skillet over medium heat. Drain shrimp; add to skillet. Stir 2 minutes. Add tomatoes, garlic and remaining 1 cup wine and simmer until shrimp are just opaque in center, about 2 minutes. Season to taste with salt and pepper.

Drain pasta; divide among large shallow bowls. Using tongs, place shrimp atop pasta. Boil sauce in skillet until thickened slightly, about 2 minutes. Spoon sauce over shrimp. Sprinkle with basil.

Fettuccine with Artichokes, Sun-dried Tomatoes and Walnuts

Toasted baguette slices topped with purchased pesto or caponata is a quick starter; a salad of mixed greens and sliced red onions is perfect alongside the pasta.

VARIATION: Try a tubular pasta, such as penne, instead of fettuccine.

---

1 pound fettuccine

1 cup coarsely chopped walnuts

2 6-ounce jars marinated quartered artichoke hearts, drained, marinade reserved

1 cup dry white wine

½ cup sour cream

1 cup chopped drained oil-packed sun-dried tomatoes (about 4 ounces)

⅔ cup plus ¼ cup finely chopped chives or green onion tops

Cook fettuccine in large pot of boiling salted water until tender but still firm to bite, stirring occasionally. Drain pasta, reserving ½ cup cooking liquid.

Meanwhile, stir walnuts in heavy large skillet over medium-high heat until lightly toasted, about 2 minutes. Transfer nuts to small plate. Pour artichoke marinade and wine into same skillet. Boil until reduced to 1 cup, about 4 minutes. Whisk in sour cream and remove from heat (do not boil). Mix in artichokes, tomatoes and ⅔ cup chopped chives.

Add pasta to sauce. Toss to blend well, adding reserved pasta cooking liquid by tablespoonfuls if pasta is dry. Season to taste with salt and pepper. Divide pasta among plates. Sprinkle with toasted walnuts and remaining ¼ cup chopped chives and serve.

Linguine with Spicy Tomato and Clam Sauce

Canned tomatoes make the pasta sauce easy to prepare, while the option of using canned clams makes this dish especially convenient.

VARIATION: Fresh mussels can stand in for the clams.

6 SERVINGS

2 28-ounce cans Italian plum tomatoes, drained

8 tablespoons olive oil

1 red onion, chopped

6 large garlic cloves, minced

½ teaspoon dried crushed red pepper

¼ cup chopped fresh marjoram or
  2 teaspoons dried

¼ cup chopped fresh Italian parsley

2 pounds fresh clams or 3 10-ounce cans whole
  baby clams, drained, 1 cup liquid reserved

1½ pounds linguine

Gently squeeze tomatoes to remove juices, then chop. Heat 6 tablespoons oil in heavy large saucepan over medium heat. Add onion and sauté until tender, about 5 minutes. Add garlic and sauté until soft, about 4 minutes. Add dried red pepper and stir 20 seconds. Mix in tomatoes and simmer until sauce thickens, stirring frequently, about 5 minutes. Season with salt and pepper. Stir in half of marjoram and half of parsley. Add clams to sauce. (Add 1 cup reserved clam liquid if using canned clams.) Cover and cook sauce until clams open, about 5 minutes.

Meanwhile, cook linguine in large pot of boiling salted water until tender but still firm to bite. Drain well. Transfer to large bowl. Add remaining 2 tablespoons oil and toss to coat. Pour clams and sauce over, discarding any clams that do not open. Sprinkle with remaining herbs.

Penne with Sausage and Tomato Sauce

A simple pasta dish like this can be put together any night of the week with pantry staples and sausages, which defrost quickly if frozen.

VARIATION: Try this sauce over any favorite pasta—rigatoni and rotini would be especially good. A pound of lean ground beef would work in place of the sausage.
DO-AHEAD: Note that this sauce can be frozen up to a month.

---

1 tablespoon olive oil

1 medium onion, chopped

4 Italian hot sausages, casings removed

¼ teaspoon dried crushed red pepper

⅓ cup red wine

1 28-ounce can crushed tomatoes with
added puree

2 teaspoons dried marjoram

1 pound penne pasta

Freshly grated Parmesan or Romano cheese

Heat oil in heavy large saucepan over medium heat. Add onion and sauté until tender, about 8 minutes. Add sausages and cook until no longer pink, breaking up with fork, about 6 minutes. Stir in dried red pepper. Add red wine and boil until absorbed. Mix in crushed tomatoes. Bring to boil, reduce heat and simmer 25 minutes. Stir marjoram into sauce. (Can be made ahead. Seal in airtight container and refrigerate up to 2 days or freeze 1 month. Bring to simmer before continuing.)

Cook penne in large pot of boiling salted water until tender but still firm to bite, stirring occasionally. Drain well. Return penne to pot. Add sauce and stir to coat. Season to taste with salt and pepper. Transfer to large bowl. Serve, passing Parmesan cheese separately.

Fettuccine with Pesto and Roasted Red Peppers

Purchased pesto and roasted peppers from a jar (two items to keep on hand) give this pasta plenty of flavor—without adding any extra work for the cook.

VARIATION: Try using ¾ cup thinly sliced oil-packed sun-dried tomatoes in place of the roasted red peppers. Any long pasta would work, too.

---

4 SERVINGS

1 pound fettuccine

2 tablespoons olive oil

2 7-ounce jars roasted red peppers, drained, rinsed, sliced

1 7-ounce package purchased pesto

Freshly grated Romano or Parmesan cheese

Cook fettuccine in large pot of boiling salted water until tender but still firm to bite, stirring occasionally.

Meanwhile, heat oil in heavy small skillet over medium-low heat. Add peppers and stir until heated through. Drain fettuccine well. Return to pot. Mix in peppers and pesto. Season to taste with salt and pepper. Serve fettuccine, passing cheese separately.

Spaghetti with Olive Oil, Garlic and Anchovies

This simple dish is based on pantry staples; some chopped parsley gives it a fresh taste.

VARIATION: This garlicky combination would work well on any favorite pasta.

DO-AHEAD: Note that the garlic-anchovy mixture can be prepared ahead of time. Cook the pasta just before dinner, toss with the sauce and serve.

4 SERVINGS

½ cup olive oil

6 to 8 large garlic cloves, minced

2 1¾- or 2-ounce cans anchovy fillets, drained, chopped

1 pound spaghetti

2 teaspoons fresh lemon juice

Chopped fresh Italian parsley

Freshly grated Parmesan cheese

Heat oil in heavy medium skillet over low heat. Add garlic and cook 2 minutes. Add anchovies and cook until garlic just begins to color, about 3 minutes. *(Can be prepared 4 hours ahead; cover and refrigerate.)*

Meanwhile, cook spaghetti in large pot of boiling salted water until tender but still firm to bite, stirring occasionally. Drain well. Return spaghetti to pot. Add anchovy mixture and lemon juice and toss to coat. Season to taste with pepper. Divide among plates. Sprinkle generously with parsley. Serve spaghetti, passing grated Parmesan cheese separately.

MIX-AND-MATCH PASTAS

Preparing the same five dinners over and over can get boring—for the cook and everyone else. Expanding your recipe repertoire doesn't have to mean making dishes that are difficult or exotic; it simply means trying something new. A good place to start experimenting is with pasta: It's easy to make, the variations are endless, and everyone loves it. Keep these ingredients on hand and mix and match as you please for ever-changing pasta suppers.

- A variety of pasta shapes: large (ziti, rigatoni); medium (penne, farfalle); long (spaghetti, linguine); wide (lasagna); small (orzo).
- Canned whole tomatoes (plum tomatoes are the best).
- Canned chopped tomatoes.
- Tomato paste.
- Canned anchovies and anchovy paste.
- Canned clams.
- Canned chicken, beef and vegetable broth.
- Purchased pesto.
- Sun-dried tomatoes.
- Olive oil.
- Grated Parmesan cheese.
- Onions and garlic.
- Fresh Italian parsley.
- Prosciutto.

Linguine with Bacon, Tomatoes and Cream

Serve this rich-tasting pasta entrée with a crisp salad of greens and artichoke hearts.

VARIATION: This sauce would also be delicious tossed with cooked purchased cheese tortellini.

1 tablespoon olive oil	8 ounces linguine
4 bacon slices, chopped	¼ cup freshly grated Romano or Parmesan cheese
2 large shallots, chopped	2 tablespoons pine nuts, toasted
½ cup whipping cream	Minced fresh Italian parsley
¼ cup sliced drained oil-packed sun-dried tomatoes	Additional freshly grated Romano or Parmesan cheese

Heat oil in heavy large skillet over medium heat. Add bacon and cook until beginning to color, about 6 minutes. Drain off fat. Add shallots and stir 1 minute. Add whipping cream and bring to boil. Turn off heat and add sliced sun-dried tomatoes.

Meanwhile, cook linguine in large pot of boiling salted water until tender but still firm to bite, stirring occasionally. Drain well. Return linguine to pot. Add sauce and ¼ cup Romano cheese and stir to coat. Season to taste with salt and pepper. Divide between plates. Sprinkle each serving with nuts and parsley. Serve, passing additional Romano cheese separately.

Farfalle with Bitter Greens and Sausage

Mustard greens and sausage give this pasta dish a hearty quality that makes it perfect for colder months. Serve with breadsticks.

VARIATION: Many kinds of greens—Swiss chard, broccoli *rabe* (also called rapini), escarole or kale, to name a few—would work well in this dish.

DO-AHEAD: The pasta sauce can be made up to four hours ahead.

---

2 tablespoons olive oil

2 large onions, chopped

6 Italian hot sausages, casings removed

4 garlic cloves, minced

2 large bunches mustard greens, stems trimmed, cut crosswise into 2-inch pieces (about 8 cups cut)

⅔ cup whipping cream

1 pound farfalle pasta

1 cup freshly grated Romano cheese

Additional freshly grated Romano cheese

4 TO 6 SERVINGS

Heat oil in heavy large skillet over medium heat. Add onions and sauté until soft, stirring occasionally, about 8 minutes. Add sausages and garlic. Cook until sausages are no longer pink, breaking up with fork, about 6 minutes. Add greens and stir until just wilted, about 3 minutes. Add cream and boil until slightly thickened, about 2 minutes. *(Can be prepared 4 hours ahead. Cover and refrigerate. Bring sauce to simmer before continuing with recipe.)*

Meanwhile, cook pasta in large pot of boiling salted water until tender but still firm to bite, stirring occasionally. Drain well; return pasta to pot. Mix in sauce and 1 cup Romano. Season to taste with salt and pepper. Serve, passing additional Romano separately.

Big Salads

Warm nights call for cool dinners, ideally big, fresh and filling salads that need only a loaf of crusty bread to round out one of the simplest of meals.

Salad Bar Cobb

Dinner is as easy as a trip to the nearest salad bar, where you'll find all the ingredients for this fast and easy version of a salad classic.

VARIATION: Substitute your favorite purchased salad dressing for the homemade one here.
DO-AHEAD: The dressing can be prepared four hours ahead of time.

½ cup extra-virgin olive oil

3 tablespoons red wine vinegar

1 tablespoon chopped fresh chives

2 teaspoons honey-Dijon mustard

2 teaspoons Worcestershire sauce

2 4½-ounce packages baby greens

2 cups diced smoked turkey or chicken
(about 10 ounces)

2 cups diced plum tomatoes

1½ cups diced avocados

1 cup chopped peeled hard-boiled eggs

1 cup crumbled cooked bacon

1 cup crumbled blue cheese

4 TO 6 SERVINGS

Whisk first 5 ingredients in small bowl to blend. Season dressing with salt and pepper. *(Dressing can be prepared up to 4 hours ahead. Cover and let stand at room temperature.)*

Divide greens among plates. Place rows of turkey, tomatoes and avocados atop greens. Sprinkle each salad with eggs, bacon and blue cheese. Drizzle salads with dressing; toss if desired.

Tossed Pizza Salad

Favorite pizza toppings—and even cubes of pizza crust—are mixed with arugula and Italian dressing in this delicious and inventive salad. Buy marinated green and black olives from the deli to serve as an appetizer.

VARIATION: Diced smoked turkey, salami or ham could be added to this salad to make it even heartier—or in the true pizza tradition, add some chopped canned anchovies.

4 SERVINGS

2 6-inch purchased fully baked pizza crusts from
  one 8-ounce package, cubed

3 cups diced tomatoes

1 cup thinly sliced fresh basil

1 cup purchased Italian dressing

2 small green bell peppers, chopped

2 cups diced fresh mozzarella cheese
  (about 8 ounces)

1 3.5-ounce package sliced pepperoni

2 large bunches arugula, stemmed, or
  half a 7-ounce bag

Toss pizza crusts, tomatoes, basil and ½ cup dressing in large bowl; let stand 5 minutes. Mix in chopped bell peppers, cheese, pepperoni and arugula. Add remaining ½ cup dressing; toss to combine. Season salad to taste with salt and pepper and serve.

Southwest Succotash Salad

Succotash, the traditional southern side dish of lima beans and corn kernels, is the inspiration for this salad. Serve it with corn tortillas and purchased salsa.

VARIATION: Two crumbled cooked bacon slices would make a flavorful addition to this salad.   2 SERVINGS

---

4 cups mixed baby greens

8 tablespoons (or more) purchased oil and
vinegar dressing

1 15- to 16-ounce can kidney beans, drained

1 cup fresh corn kernels, cut from
2 small ears of corn

1 cup ½-inch pieces hot pepper Monterey Jack
cheese (about 4 ounces)

1 small red bell pepper, cut into 1-inch-long strips

⅓ cup chopped fresh cilantro

1 teaspoon ground cumin

Divide greens between 2 large shallow bowls.
Drizzle each serving with 1 tablespoon dressing.
Combine 6 tablespoons dressing and remaining
ingredients in medium bowl and toss to coat,
adding more dressing if desired. Season to taste
with salt and pepper. Mound salad atop greens
in bowls and then serve.

SALAD TIPS

Thanks to the proliferation of farmers' markets across the country, salads have never been fresher. And thanks to pre-washed lettuces in bags, they've never been easier, either. Add a few choice leftovers and dinner is practically done. Keep these things in mind when you're making a salad supper.

- Assertive Greens: When you're using the likes of watercress, arugula, radicchio and dandelion greens, use similarly assertive meats, cheeses and vegetables (such as smoked sausages, Gorgonzola and radishes). Dressings should also be bold. Try those made with balsamic vinegar, anchovy paste and nut oils.

- Delicate Greens: When using Boston or Bibb lettuce or *mâche*, choose foods that are subtle in flavor and elegant in texture, such as poached chicken, steamed lobster or grilled shrimp. Dressings should not be overwhelming. Try those made with rice vinegar, Champagne vinegar and mild olive oil.

- Herbs: Fresh herbs are a delicious addition to salads. The trick is to not mix too many different kinds in one salad. Try thinly sliced strips of basil in Mediterranean-inspired salads, chopped cilantro in salads with Asian or Tex-Mex flavors, and snipped fresh chives or dill in chicken, fish or shellfish salads.

- Vegetables: In addition to the expected lettuce, add seasonal vegetables. Steamed asparagus, snow peas, green beans and just about any grilled vegetable make good additions.

Mediterranean Salad

Stuffed grape leaves, marinated mushrooms and pita bread from the deli would make a delicious Mediterranean-themed meal centered on this salad.

VARIATION: Add chopped prosciutto or shredded chicken to make the salad heartier.

4 SERVINGS

1 cup purchased balsamic vinaigrette

6 tablespoons chopped fresh mint

2 15-ounce cans garbanzo beans (chickpeas), drained

10 ounces mixed baby greens

2 large oranges, peeled, sliced into thin rounds

2 cups diced feta cheese or one 1.7-ounce package, crumbled

1 cup pitted Kalamata olives or other brine-cured black olives

Whisk vinaigrette and mint in large bowl to blend; mix in garbanzo beans. Set beans aside for 10 minutes. Add mixed baby greens to bean mixture in bowl and toss to coat. Divide salad among large plates. Top with orange rounds, diced feta cheese and olives and serve.

White Bean and Tuna Salad

For a simple starter, thinly slice and toast a French bread baguette and top each slice with chopped tomatoes tossed with olive oil and chopped fresh basil.

4 SERVINGS

2 15-ounce cans cannellini (white kidney beans), rinsed, drained

2 12½-ounce cans white tuna, drained

2 large tomatoes, seeded, diced

½ cup chopped red onion

2 tablespoons fresh lemon juice

1½ tablespoons Dijon mustard

½ cup olive oil

½ cup chopped fresh basil

Lettuce leaves

Whole fresh basil leaves

Toss beans, tuna, tomatoes and onion in large bowl to combine. Whisk lemon juice and mustard in small bowl to blend. Gradually whisk in oil. Add to salad. Mix in chopped basil. Season with salt and pepper. *(Can be prepared 8 hours ahead. Cover and refrigerate.)* Line plates with lettuce leaves. Spoon salad onto lettuce. Garnish with whole basil leaves and serve.

Curried Chicken, Green Bean and Almond Salad

Indian flavors like curry, cilantro and yogurt give the classic chicken salad a new twist.

VARIATION: This salad can be made with shredded roast turkey instead of chicken. Raisins would be a good addition.

DO-AHEAD: Make the salad in the morning, if you like.

---

12 ounces green beans, trimmed, halved crosswise	2 teaspoons curry powder	4 SERVINGS
2 cups shredded roasted chicken breast meat (from about 3 chicken breast halves)	⅓ cup plain yogurt	
1 cup thinly sliced red onion	3 tablespoons mayonnaise	
5 tablespoons chopped fresh cilantro	1 tablespoon fresh lime juice	
	2 tablespoons sliced almonds, toasted	

Cook beans in pot of boiling salted water until crisp-tender, about 5 minutes. Drain and rinse under cold water. Drain well. Transfer beans to large bowl. Add chicken, onion and 4 tablespoons cilantro.

Stir curry powder in small skillet over medium heat until aromatic, about 30 seconds. Transfer to small bowl. Whisk in yogurt, mayonnaise and lime juice. Add dressing to chicken mixture; toss to coat. Season to taste with salt and pepper. *(Can be made 8 hours ahead. Cover and refrigerate.)* Sprinkle with almonds and remaining 1 tablespoon cilantro.

Santa Fe Pork Salad
with Guacamole Dressing

Serve the salad in tostada shells, or pass a basket of warm corn tortillas to go with it.

DO-AHEAD: Note that both the pork and the guacamole dressing can be prepared ahead. The salad is put together and drizzled with dressing just before serving.

4 SERVINGS

1¼ cups (about 10 ounces) purchased guacamole
    or avocado dip
6 tablespoons fresh lime juice

1 pound stir-fry/fajita-cut pork strips or 1 pound
    wafer-thin boneless pork loin chops, cut into
    generous ¼-inch-thick strips

2½ teaspoons ground cumin
2 tablespoons vegetable oil

8 cups packaged salad greens
1 cup drained canned black beans, rinsed
    Purchased salsa

Whisk guacamole and lime juice in small bowl to blend; season dressing to taste with salt and pepper. *(Can be prepared 2 hours ahead. Cover and refrigerate.)*

Sprinkle pork on all sides with cumin, salt and pepper. Heat oil in heavy large skillet over medium-high heat. Add pork and sauté until brown and cooked through, about 4 minutes. Transfer pork to plate. *(Can be prepared 20 minutes ahead. Let stand at room temperature.)*

Divide salad greens among shallow bowls. Top each salad with ¼ of black beans and ¼ of pork and any pan juices. Drizzle some dressing over each salad and top each with dollop of salsa. Serve salads, passing remaining dressing separately.

Chicken and Caponata Salad

Caponata, a flavorful relish of eggplants, tomatoes, onions, anchovies, olives, pine nuts, capers, vinegar and olive oil, is sold canned. Check the local deli for a fresh version. Pick up a good loaf of bread while you're there, and have slices of angel food cake with whipped cream and raspberries for dessert.

VARIATION: The escarole can be replaced with a five-ounce bag of mixed greens or one bunch of arugula and one large head of radicchio.

4 TO 6 SERVINGS

1 medium head escarole, torn into bite-size pieces	¼ cup plus 4 teaspoons balsamic vinegar
10 tablespoons olive oil	2 tablespoons grated orange peel
6 skinless boneless chicken breast halves	1 tablespoon Dijon mustard
2 large shallots, minced	
½ cup fresh orange juice	2 7½-ounce cans purchased caponata

Place escarole in large bowl. Heat 2 tablespoons oil in heavy large skillet over medium-low heat. Sprinkle chicken with salt and pepper. Add to skillet and sauté until cooked through, about 5 minutes per side. Transfer to plate. Add shallots to skillet and stir 1 minute. Add orange juice and ¼ cup vinegar and boil until reduced to glaze. Remove from heat. Whisk in orange peel, mustard and remaining 4 teaspoons vinegar. Gradually whisk in remaining 8 tablespoons oil. Season with salt and pepper.

Cut chicken into pieces. Add chicken and caponata to escarole. Add dressing; toss to coat.

Shrimp, Potato and Cucumber Salad with Dill Dressing

A quick and easy one-dish meal. All you need to go with it is some Swedish rye bread.

DO-AHEAD: Note that this salad can be prepared up to four hours ahead, and it's served cold or at room temperature, so no last-minute preparation is required.

2 SERVINGS

4 medium-size red-skinned new potatoes,
cut into ¾-inch pieces

1½ tablespoons Dijon mustard

1 tablespoon white wine vinegar

⅓ cup olive oil

3 green onions, chopped

1 tablespoon minced fresh dill

4 pickling cucumbers, halved lengthwise and sliced
crosswise (about 1½ cups)

½ pound cooked bay shrimp

Cook potatoes in medium pot of boiling water until just tender, about 15 minutes. Drain well. Place in large bowl. Combine mustard and vinegar in small bowl. Gradually whisk in oil. Add half of dressing to warm potatoes. Mix in green onions and dill; season with salt and pepper. Cool completely. Add cucumbers, shrimp and remaining dressing and toss to coat. Season to taste with salt and pepper. *(Can be prepared 4 hours ahead. Cover and refrigerate.)*

Macaroni, Tomato, Corn and Basil Salad

Ripe tomatoes, basil and fresh corn make this a terrific summer salad.

VARIATION: Small shell-shaped pasta would be great in this salad. Nonfat yogurt and low-fat mayonnaise can be used to make a lighter version.

DO-AHEAD: This recipe can be made several hours ahead, covered, refrigerated and served cold or at room temperature.

¾ cup uncooked elbow macaroni (about 3½ ounces)

4 medium tomatoes, cut into thin wedges

5 green onions, thinly sliced

1 cup thin slices halved English hothouse cucumber

1 cup fresh corn kernels or frozen, thawed

1 cup (packed) fresh basil leaves

⅓ cup plain yogurt

3 tablespoons mayonnaise

1½ tablespoons fresh lime juice

2 garlic cloves, peeled

2 SERVINGS

Cook macaroni in medium saucepan of boiling salted water until tender but still firm to bite. Drain. Rinse under cold water. Drain well. Transfer macaroni to large bowl. Add tomato wedges, sliced green onions, cucumber slices and corn kernels.

Blend basil, yogurt, mayonnaise, lime juice and garlic in processor until basil is finely chopped. Add basil dressing to macaroni mixture and toss to blend. Season salad to taste with salt and pepper. *(Can be prepared 4 hours ahead. Cover and refrigerate.)*

Dinner-in-a-Bowl Soups

It's been a long day, it's late in the evening and the cook is worn out. What's needed for dinner is soup—a big, warming bowl of something comforting, quick-simmering and easy.

Summer Garden Soup

As the name indicates, this simple soup is a perfect use for a bumper crop of summer squash and vine-ripened tomatoes. Serve it with garlic bread.

VARIATION: Pancetta would be good in place of the ham. For a meatless version of the soup, leave out the ham, add an extra can of beans, and use vegetable stock.

---

2 tablespoons olive oil

2 medium onions, chopped

2 small zucchini

2 small yellow crookneck squash

2 15-ounce cans cannellini (white kidney beans), undrained

2 14½-ounce cans low-salt chicken broth

½ pound diced ham

2 medium tomatoes, seeded, chopped

1 7-ounce package purchased pesto

4 SERVINGS

Heat oil in heavy large saucepan over medium-low heat. Add onions and sauté until translucent, about 8 minutes. Cut zucchini and squash lengthwise into fourths, then slice. Add to saucepan and season with pepper. Cook until crisp-tender, stirring occasionally, about 6 minutes. Remove from heat. Mix in beans with their liquid, broth, ham and tomatoes. *(Can be prepared 3 hours ahead. Cover and refrigerate.)* Mix in 2 tablespoons pesto. Cool to room temperature or bring to simmer. Ladle into bowls. Swirl additional pesto into each bowl and serve.

Quick Black Bean Soup

Top bowls of this soup with dollops of sour cream and some chopped fresh cilantro before serving, if you like. Cheese quesadillas would round out the meal.

VARIATION: Use canned vegetable broth instead of chicken broth for a vegetarian version.
DO-AHEAD: Note that this soup keeps well in the refrigerator; it also freezes well. Seal in an airtight container and freeze up to a week.

6 SERVINGS

2 tablespoons olive oil	2 14½-ounce cans low-salt chicken broth
1¼ cups chopped onion	1 28-ounce can diced tomatoes in juice
4 large garlic cloves, chopped	2 teaspoons ground cumin
1 tablespoon chopped fresh thyme or	1½ teaspoons hot pepper sauce
1½ teaspoons dried	
3 15-ounce cans black beans, drained,	
1 cup liquid reserved	

Heat oil in large pot over medium heat. Add onion, garlic and thyme; sauté until onion is golden, about 8 minutes. Add beans, reserved 1 cup bean liquid, broth, tomatoes with juices, cumin and hot pepper sauce. Bring soup to boil. Reduce heat to medium-low and simmer until flavors blend and soup thickens slightly, stirring occasionally, about 20 minutes.

Working in 2 batches, puree 2½ cups soup in blender until smooth. Mix puree back into soup in pot. Season to taste with salt and pepper. *(Can be prepared 3 days ahead. Cover and refrigerate. Bring to simmer before serving.)* Ladle soup into bowls.

Broccoli and Cauliflower Cheese Soup with Sausage

This hearty soup makes a comforting cold-weather entrée. Serve with sourdough rolls.

DO-AHEAD: This soup can be partially prepared ahead; adding the dairy ingredients and the broccoli and cauliflower just before serving insures that the soup will keep well and that the vegetables will still be crisp-tender when it's served.

¼ cup (½ stick) butter

8 ounces smoked beef sausage or kielbasa, quartered lengthwise, sliced crosswise

2 medium onions, chopped

1 teaspoon caraway seeds, crushed

2 pounds russet potatoes, peeled, sliced

4 14½-ounce cans low-salt chicken broth

1 bay leaf

3 cups bite-size broccoli florets

3 cups bite-size cauliflower florets

½ cup whipping cream

6 ounces sharp cheddar cheese, grated

Additional crushed caraway seeds

Melt butter in heavy large saucepan over medium heat. Add sausage and sauté until beginning to brown, about 4 minutes. Using slotted spoon, remove sausage from pan. Add onions and 1 teaspoon caraway seeds. Sprinkle with pepper. Reduce heat to medium-low and cook 4 minutes, stirring occasionally. Mix in potatoes. Add broth and bay leaf. Simmer until potatoes are tender, stirring occasionally and breaking up potatoes with spoon, about 25 minutes. *(Can be prepared 1 day ahead. Cover and refrigerate sausage and soup separately. Bring soup to simmer over medium heat before continuing.)*

Add broccoli and cauliflower to soup and simmer until just tender, about 10 minutes. Stir in cream and sausage; simmer until heated through. Add cheese and mix until melted. Season to taste with salt and pepper. Discard bay leaf. Ladle into bowls. Sprinkle with caraway seeds and serve.

Mediterranean Seafood and Orzo Soup

Serve this soup with French bread toasts topped with chopped marinated artichoke hearts that have been tossed with a little olive oil.

VARIATION: Any very small pasta, such as *riso,* would work well in place of the orzo in this soup; red snapper can be used instead of halibut.

4 SERVINGS

1½ pounds halibut, cut into 1-inch cubes

3 tablespoons fresh lemon juice

4 teaspoons plus ¼ cup olive oil

2 large onions, halved, thinly sliced

1 28-ounce can Italian plum tomatoes, drained

4 8-ounce bottles clam juice

1½ cups dry white wine

1 bay leaf

2 1x4-inch orange peel strips

¼ teaspoon fennel seeds, crushed

¼ teaspoon dried crushed red pepper

1 cup orzo

2 pounds fresh clams, well scrubbed, or

two 10-ounce cans whole baby clams, drained

Minced fresh parsley

Mix halibut, lemon juice and 4 teaspoons oil in medium bowl. Let mixture stand while preparing soup.

Heat ¼ cup oil in heavy large saucepan over medium heat. Add onions and cook until translucent, stirring occasionally, about 10 minutes. Squeeze tomatoes through fingers to break up while adding to saucepan. Add clam juice, wine, bay leaf, orange peel strips, fennel and dried red pepper. Simmer soup for 10 minutes. Add orzo and cook 5 minutes.

Add clams to soup. Cover and cook 5 minutes. Add halibut. Cover and cook until halibut is opaque and clams open, about 4 minutes longer. Discard bay leaf, orange peel and any clams that do not open. Season to taste with salt and pepper. Spoon soup into bowls. Garnish with parsley.

Gazpacho with Sautéed Scallops

If you plan to serve this right away, start with chilled vegetables and tomato juice.

VARIATION: Shrimp make a good alternative to scallops; use 2¼ pounds peeled deveined shrimp and sauté them as you would the scallops.

DO-AHEAD: The soup can be made a day ahead of time, but be sure to sauté the scallops (or shrimp) shortly before serving.

---

3 cucumbers, peeled, halved lengthwise, seeded

3 green bell peppers, halved, seeded

2 small red onions, cut into 1-inch pieces

6 cups tomato juice

¾ cup plus 3 tablespoons olive oil

½ cup red wine vinegar

½ teaspoon hot pepper sauce

2¼ pounds sea scallops, halved

Minced fresh cilantro

Coarsely chop 1½ cucumbers and 1½ bell peppers. Place in processor with onions. Add tomato juice and process until coarse puree forms. Add ¾ cup oil, vinegar and hot pepper sauce and blend. Transfer to large bowl. Season to taste with salt and pepper. Cut remaining cucumbers and bell peppers into ⅓-inch cubes and add to soup. *(Can be prepared 1 day ahead; cover with plastic wrap and refrigerate.)* Divide soup among bowls.

Heat remaining 3 tablespoons oil in heavy large skillet over high heat. Add scallops. Sprinkle with salt and pepper. Sauté until just opaque, about 2 minutes. Divide scallops among bowls. Top with minced fresh cilantro and then serve immediately.

Bacon and White Bean Soup

Toast thin slices of French bread baguette, brush with olive oil, top with blue cheese and broil briefly for a perfect accompaniment to this soup.

VARIATION: Six ounces of prosciutto or half a pound of Italian hot sausages with the casings removed can be substituted for the bacon here.

DO-AHEAD: This recipe can be prepared up to two days ahead of time.

4 SERVINGS

8 slices bacon, chopped

2 medium onions, chopped

1 medium cabbage head, thinly sliced crosswise

¼ teaspoon dried crushed red pepper

3 14½-ounce cans (or more) low-salt chicken broth

4 15-ounce cans cannellini (white kidney beans), drained, rinsed

1 teaspoon dried rubbed sage

Minced fresh parsley

Sauté bacon in heavy medium saucepan until crisp. Using slotted spoon, transfer to paper towels to drain. Add chopped onions to pan and sauté over medium heat until translucent, stirring occasionally, approximately 10 minutes.

Add cabbage to saucepan and cook until tender, stirring frequently, about 8 minutes. Mix in dried red pepper, then 3 cans broth. Stir in beans and sage. Simmer 15 minutes, stirring occasionally. Season to taste with salt and pepper. *(Can be prepared 2 days ahead. Cover and refrigerate. Rewarm over medium-low heat, stirring frequently and thinning with additional chicken broth if necessary.)* Ladle soup into bowls. Sprinkle with bacon and parsley and serve.

Chicken Soup Verde

The *verde* part of this recipe comes from the green vegetables in it—asparagus, peas and green onions. Melon slices and prosciutto make a great beginning to this meal.

VARIATION: *Haricots verts* or stringed sugar snap peas can replace the asparagus.
DO-AHEAD: Make the soup a day ahead, if you like.

4 SERVINGS

6 cups canned low-salt chicken broth

2 cups dry white wine

4 skinless boneless chicken breast halves,
   cut into ½-inch pieces

16 thin asparagus spears, trimmed, cut diagonally
   into 1-inch pieces

1 cup shelled fresh peas or frozen petite peas

1 cup thinly sliced green onions

2 teaspoons chopped fresh marjoram or
   ½ teaspoon dried

1½ cups grated Parmesan cheese

Bring broth and wine to boil in heavy large saucepan over medium-high heat. Add chicken, asparagus and peas. Reduce heat and simmer until chicken is almost cooked through and vegetables are crisp-tender, about 3 minutes. Add green onions and marjoram. Simmer until chicken is cooked through and flavors blend, 2 minutes longer. *(Can be prepared 1 day ahead. Cover and refrigerate. Bring to simmer before continuing.)* Mix ½ cup Parmesan into soup; season to taste with salt and pepper. Ladle soup into bowls. Serve, passing remaining Parmesan.

SOUP TOPPERS

Few would contest that a bowl of soup, a thick slice of toasted French bread and a glass of wine make a fine dinner indeed. An extra flourish—a topping, a garnish—can add flavor and texture to that soup without much extra effort.

- Capers: Coarsely chop these peppery buds and sprinkle them on minestrone or other soups with Mediterranean flavor.
- Cheese: Grate Parmesan on minestrone or bean soups; use cheddar or Monterey Jack on vegetable or tomato soups.
- Croutons: Homemade croutons are a real treat. They're as simple as sautéing cubes of stale bread in olive oil or butter until golden. Sprinkle them on creamy soups and vegetable purees.
- Eggs: Hard-boil eggs and then chop them. Sprinkle on bean soups, gazpacho and vegetable soups.
- Ham and Bacon: A spoonful of crumbled, cooked bacon or sautéed, julienne ham or prosciutto is delicious on creamy soups, especially those made with legumes and peas.
- Herbs: Use the same herbs to garnish the soup that went into its preparation. Herb flowers are a pretty addition, too.
- Nuts: Toast and chop hazelnuts, pecans or walnuts and try them on soups made with winter squash or sweet potatoes.
- Roasted Red Peppers: Chop and sprinkle on vegetable soups or Mediterranean-themed soups.

Smoked Sausage, Kale and Potato Soup

A romaine and beet salad and whole-grain rolls complete the meal.

VARIATION: Try spinach in place of the kale.
DO-AHEAD: This can be stored in the refrigerator for two days.

4 SERVINGS

½ pound smoked fully cooked sausage (such as kielbasa or hot links), sliced into rounds

5½ cups canned low-salt chicken broth

1½ pounds small red-skinned new potatoes, thinly sliced

2 cups dry white wine

10 cups thinly sliced trimmed kale leaves or 1½ ten-ounce packages frozen chopped kale, thawed, drained

½ teaspoon caraway seeds, lightly crushed

Sauté sausage slices in heavy large saucepan over medium-high heat until beginning to brown, about 3 minutes. Add chicken broth, sliced potatoes and white wine and bring mixture to boil. Reduce heat to medium, cover and simmer until potatoes are almost tender, about 10 minutes.

Add kale and caraway seeds to soup. Simmer soup uncovered until potatoes and kale are very tender, about 10 minutes longer. *(Can be prepared 2 days ahead. Let stand until cool, then cover and refrigerate. Bring to simmer before continuing.)* Season soup to taste with salt and pepper. Ladle soup into bowls and serve immediately.

Vegetarian Tortilla Soup

Pair this southwestern-style soup with leaves of romaine lettuce topped with purchased guacamole or salsa and a plate of quesadillas or nachos.

DO-AHEAD: Get started on this soup a day ahead, if you like.

Nonstick vegetable oil spray

¾ cup chopped onion

2 garlic cloves, minced

1 tablespoon tomato paste

1 teaspoon ground cumin

¾ teaspoon chili powder

4 cups canned vegetable broth

4 tablespoons chopped fresh cilantro

4 6-inch-diameter corn tortillas, cut into
   ½-inch-wide strips

1½ cups chopped tomatoes

⅔ cup canned black beans or pinto beans,
   drained, rinsed

⅔ cup chopped zucchini

1½ tablespoons minced seeded jalapeño chili

Spray large nonstick saucepan with nonstick spray. Add onion and garlic; cover and cook over medium-low heat until almost tender, stirring often, about 5 minutes. Stir in tomato paste, cumin and chili powder. Add broth and 2 tablespoons cilantro; bring to boil. Reduce heat; cover and simmer until flavors blend, 15 minutes. *(Can be made 1 day ahead; chill. Bring to simmer before continuing.)*

Add tortillas, tomatoes, beans, zucchini and jalapeño to soup. Cover; simmer until zucchini is tender, about 5 minutes. Season to taste with salt and pepper.

Ladle soup into bowls. Sprinkle with remaining 2 tablespoons cilantro and serve.

Sandwich Suppers

Two slices of bread, a savory spread and something in the middle—sandwiches are wonderfully simple and satisfying. They are also as easy as dinner gets.

Turkey Cheeseburgers

Serve these the way you like your burgers best—on rolls or buns or alone, with all of your favorite condiments. Fries are the expected go-with.

VARIATION: Swiss or Monterey Jack cheese would also be good atop these burgers.

DO-AHEAD: To cut down on last-minute preparation time, make the patties a day ahead.

1⅓ cups fresh sourdough breadcrumbs (from about 2 large slices)	Sliced Gouda or other cheese
¼ cup minced shallots	4 hamburger buns, toasted
3½ tablespoons olive oil	Red onion slices
2 tablespoons minced fresh tarragon or 1½ teaspoons dried, crumbled	Tomato slices
½ teaspoon salt	Mixed greens
1⅓ pounds ground turkey meat	

4 SERVINGS

Mix breadcrumbs, shallots, 2½ tablespoons oil, tarragon and salt in medium bowl. Mix in ground turkey; sprinkle with pepper. Form mixture into four ½-inch-thick patties. *(Can be prepared 1 day ahead. Cover with plastic wrap and refrigerate.)*

Heat 1 tablespoon oil in heavy medium skillet over medium heat. Add patties. Cover and fry until just cooked through, about 3 minutes per side. Top each patty with cheese. Cover and cook until cheese is just melted. Transfer burgers to buns, adding onion, tomato and greens as desired.

Fish and Pickled Onion Sandwiches

French fries (or potato chips), coleslaw and watermelon wedges are the requisite accompaniments to these fried fish sandwiches.

VARIATION: Try orange roughy or tilapia in place of the catfish fillets for a change.

2 6-ounce catfish fillets, each cut into 3 pieces
  Yellow cornmeal
2½ tablespoons vegetable oil

1 large sweet onion (such as Vidalia or Maui),
  thinly sliced

3 tablespoons white wine vinegar
1 tablespoon chopped fresh thyme

2 kaiser rolls, split, lightly toasted
  Purchased tartar sauce

Sprinkle fish with salt and pepper, then dust with cornmeal on both sides. Heat 1½ tablespoons oil in heavy large skillet over medium-high heat. Add fish and sauté until crisp outside and just opaque in center, about 3 minutes per side. Transfer fish to plate.

Wipe out skillet with paper towels. Heat remaining 1 tablespoon oil in same skillet over medium-high heat. Add onion; sauté until beginning to color, 3 minutes. Add vinegar and thyme. Sauté until onion is golden and vinegar has evaporated, about 2 minutes. Season with salt and pepper.

Spread bottom half of rolls with tartar sauce. Top each with 3 fish pieces, onion and roll top.

Grilled Vegetable Heroes

These sandwiches go well with macaroni salad and sweet-potato chips.

VARIATION: Use thinly sliced eggplant in place of zucchini. Sprinkle eggplant slices with salt and let drain in strainer 30 minutes before brushing with oil mixture.

4 large zucchini, sliced lengthwise

2 large red bell peppers, quartered
   lengthwise, seeded

2 large firm tomatoes, cut horizontally
   into 4 slices each

12 tablespoons purchased Italian salad dressing

¼ cup chopped fresh basil plus 16 large
   whole basil leaves

4 Italian sandwich rolls with seeds, split lengthwise

8 thin slices provolone cheese

4 SERVINGS

Prepare barbecue (medium-high heat). Arrange zucchini, bell peppers and tomatoes on rimmed baking sheet. Whisk dressing and chopped basil in medium bowl to blend. Brush cut side of each roll with ½ tablespoon dressing. Brush vegetables with remaining dressing and sprinkle with salt and pepper.

Grill cut side of rolls until toasted, about 1 minute. Place rolls, cut side up, on plates. Grill vegetables until tender and lightly charred, turning and brushing occasionally with any dressing mixture left on baking sheet, about 10 minutes. Arrange warm vegetables on roll bottoms. Cover each with 2 slices cheese, 4 whole basil leaves and top of roll and serve.

Roast Beef Wraps
with Horseradish Coleslaw

Serve with purchased potato salad and raw vegetable sticks.

VARIATION: Try rolling any of your favorite sandwich fillings in a wrap. Either turkey, Jack cheese and avocado, or mozzarella, pesto and fresh tomatoes would be delicious.

2 cups purchased creamy coleslaw

3 tablespoons prepared white horseradish

3 tablespoons chopped fresh thyme or
   2 teaspoons dried

4 10-inch-diameter flour tortillas or
   two 4½-ounce sheets soft lavash bread,
   trimmed to 20-inch length

1 pound thinly sliced roast beef

2 7-ounce jars roasted red peppers, drained, sliced

1 cup chopped green onions

Stir coleslaw, horseradish and thyme in small bowl to blend. Set aside.

Heat large skillet over medium heat. Add 1 tortilla to skillet and heat until soft, about 1 minute per side; transfer to work surface. Repeat with remaining tortillas. Alternatively, open lavash on work surface. Spread ¼ of coleslaw mixture on each tortilla or half of coleslaw mixture on each lavash, leaving ½-inch border at edges. Arrange beef, roasted peppers and green onions over coleslaw mixture. Starting at edge of tortillas or at 1 long side of lavash, roll up, enclosing fillings. Cut tortillas in half or lavash into 8 pieces and then serve.

Western Club Sandwiches

The classic club sandwich is made with three slices of bread, chicken or turkey, bacon, lettuce and tomato. This version gets its western flavor from avocado, cilantro and chilies. A bean and rice salad and crunchy pickles would go well with it.

VARIATION: Ham or smoked chicken could be used instead of smoked turkey.
DO-AHEAD: These can be made hours ahead and refrigerated until ready to serve.

4 SERVINGS

⅔ cup mayonnaise

¼ cup chopped fresh cilantro

2 to 3 tablespoons minced pickled jalapeño chilies

12 slices firm whole grain bread

12 ounces thinly sliced smoked turkey

8 thin slices red onion

2 ripe avocados, peeled, sliced

2 cups radish sprouts or alfalfa sprouts

Stir mayonnaise, cilantro and jalapeños in small bowl to blend. Season dressing to taste with salt.

Place 4 bread slices on plates. Spread each with some of dressing. Top with turkey, onion, a second bread slice, remaining dressing, avocado slices and sprouts. Place third bread slice atop each sandwich; press to compact slightly. Cut sandwiches into quarters; skewer together with extra-long toothpicks. *(Can be prepared 6 hours ahead. Cover and refrigerate.)*

SANDWICH IDEAS

A dinner sandwich is not like the one you had for lunch. It is more substantial than the basic ham and cheese, and since it doesn't have to travel, pack or keep for several hours at room temperature, its ingredients can be more varied. If you're still not convinced that a sandwich can make a hearty, satisfying supper, try this tactic: Serve it open-face on a real plate with a knife and fork, a cloth napkin and a glass of wine. More tips follow.

- Leftovers: Sliced broiled steak, grilled lamb, grilled tuna, poached or grilled chicken and roasted vegetables make a welcome return to the dinner table in a hearty sandwich.
- Spreads: Mayonnaise and mustard are fine, but don't forget other possibilities, such as hummus, chutney, oil and vinegar, pesto, olive paste and purchased salad dressings.
- Crunch: Don't underestimate the appeal of crunch in a sandwich. Add it in the form of radicchio, Belgian endive, baby dandelion greens, sliced radishes or cucumbers, or grated carrots.
- Extras: Turn to the pantry for such unexpected additions as marinated mushrooms, marinated artichoke hearts, pitted black or green olives and roasted red peppers.

Seared Tuna Burgers
with Ginger-Garlic Mayonnaise

This is an elegant and easy sandwich. The tuna is cooked until just opaque; add a couple of minutes extra cooking time, if you prefer.

VARIATION: Swordfish can be used instead of tuna.

4 SERVINGS

4 ¾-inch-thick tuna steaks (each about 5 to 6 ounces)

4 teaspoons olive oil

2 tablespoons minced peeled fresh ginger

2 garlic cloves, minced

½ cup mayonnaise

2 tablespoons fresh lemon juice

4 oversize sesame-seed sandwich rolls, toasted

2 bunches arugula or watercress, stems trimmed

Sprinkle tuna with salt and pepper. Heat olive oil in heavy large skillet over medium-high heat. Add tuna to skillet and cook until brown outside and just opaque in center, about 3 minutes per side. Transfer tuna to plate. Add ginger and garlic to same skillet; stir 30 seconds. Scrape into small bowl. Mix in mayonnaise and lemon juice. Season to taste with salt and pepper.

Spread bottoms of rolls with mayonnaise mixture. Top with tuna, arugula and tops of rolls.

Chicken, Olive and Tomato Sandwiches

If olivada isn't available, puree pitted brine-cured black olives (such as Kalamata) instead.

4 SERVINGS

4 French bread demi-baguettes or 2 baguettes, halved crosswise

2 large tomatoes, sliced

Dried marjoram

2 tablespoons olive oil

4 large skinless boneless chicken breast halves

Olivada*

Mayonnaise

Mustard greens or curly endive

Preheat broiler. Halve bread lengthwise. Sprinkle tomatoes with marjoram, salt and pepper.

Heat oil in heavy medium skillet over medium heat. Sprinkle chicken with salt and pepper. Add to skillet and sauté until just cooked through, turning occasionally, about 8 minutes.

Meanwhile, broil bread cut side up until light brown. Spread bottom halves with olivada. Spread cut side of tops with mayonnaise. Arrange tomato slices over olive spread. Slice chicken thinly across grain on diagonal. Arrange atop tomato slices. Top with mustard greens. Replace top halves of bread. Halve sandwiches crosswise and serve immediately.

*Sometimes called black olive paste, olivada is available at Italian markets and specialty foods stores.

Skirt Steak, Onion and Bell Pepper Sandwiches

Skirt steak, a tender, flavorful cut of meat when properly cooked, has become popular because it's used in fajitas. Serve these sandwiches with an escarole and tomato salad.

VARIATION: Flank steak makes a good substitute for skirt steak here; wrap the sandwich fillings in warm flour tortillas for a change.

---

5 tablespoons olive oil	½ teaspoon ground cumin
2 red onions, halved, sliced	½ teaspoon dried thyme
2 medium red bell peppers, cut into thin strips	2 2.5-ounce cans sliced black olives, drained
1 pound skirt steak, cut crosswise into ¼-inch-thick strips	4 pita bread rounds, halved

4 SERVINGS

Heat 4 tablespoons oil in heavy medium skillet over medium-low heat. Add onions and bell peppers. Sauté until onions and bell peppers are very tender, about 15 minutes. Season with salt and pepper. Transfer onions and peppers to plate. *(Can be made 1 hour ahead. Let stand at room temperature.)*

Heat remaining 1 tablespoon oil in same skillet over high heat. Add steak and sprinkle with salt and pepper. Sauté until no longer pink, about 1 minute. Return vegetables to skillet. Add cumin and thyme and stir 30 seconds. Remove from heat and mix in black olives. Spoon into pita breads.

Grilled Prosciutto and Fontina Sandwiches

Serve this Italian-style ham-and-cheese sandwich with tomato soup from the deli (or with canned tomato soup garnished with chopped fresh basil).

VARIATION: Thinly sliced ham and Swiss cheese would work well in this hot sandwich.

4 SERVINGS

½ pound Fontina or Havarti cheese
8 large slices sourdough bread
12 thin slices prosciutto or cooked bacon

Fresh basil leaves

Olive oil

Thinly slice cheese. Divide half of cheese among 4 bread slices, covering completely. Cover cheese with prosciutto slices or bacon. Cover prosciutto with basil leaves, then remaining cheese. Top each sandwich with second sourdough bread slice.

Heat heavy large skillet over medium heat. Working in batches, brush one side of each sandwich with oil and sprinkle generously with pepper. Arrange oiled side down in skillet. Brush top with oil and sprinkle with pepper. Cook until bread is golden brown and cheese melts, pressing down occasionally with spatula, about 3 minutes per side. Cut each sandwich in half and serve immediately.

Mushroom Wraps with
Spinach, Bell Peppers and Goat Cheese

This vegetarian wrap—a sort of sandwich-burrito hybrid—is a healthy take on fast food.

VARIATION: Add one 15- to 16-ounce can of drained black beans to the filling for extra protein. Button or crimini mushrooms will work in place of the portobellos.

¼ cup olive oil

1½ pounds portobello mushrooms, stemmed,
    caps thinly sliced

2 14½-ounce cans Mexican-style stewed tomatoes

6 burrito-size flour tortillas

1½ cups crumbled soft fresh goat cheese
    (such as Montrachet; about 7 ounces)

12 tablespoons chopped green onions

12 tablespoons chopped fresh cilantro

2 cups sliced yellow bell peppers

2 large plum tomatoes, seeded, cut into thin strips

3 cups (lightly packed) baby spinach leaves
    (about 3 ounces)

6 SERVINGS

Heat oil in large pot over medium-high heat. Add mushrooms and sauté until tender, about 10 minutes. Add canned tomatoes with juices. Cook until liquid thickens slightly, about 15 minutes. Season mushroom mixture to taste with salt and pepper.

Heat large skillet over high heat. Add 1 tortilla to skillet and cook until soft, about 15 seconds per side. Place on work surface. Spoon ⅙ of mushroom mixture in strip on lower half, leaving 2-inch border at sides. Top with ¼ cup cheese, 2 tablespoons onions, 2 tablespoons cilantro, ⅙ of peppers and tomatoes, then ½ cup spinach leaves. Fold in sides of tortilla over filling; fold up bottom and continue to roll up, enclosing filling. Repeat with remaining tortillas and filling.

Baked Potatoes and Beyond

Baked potatoes make the perfect foil for almost anywhere your culinary imagination takes you: Add the likes of cheese and bacon, spicy chili, or a bunch of south-of-the-border tastes, and dinner is done.

Mexican-Style Stuffed Potatoes

Toss greens with roasted red peppers, corn and a lime vinaigrette to serve with the potatoes.

VARIATION: Try using pepper Jack for a spicier version of this recipe.

DO-AHEAD: These can be prepared a couple of hours ahead of time but not much longer than that—the tortilla chips will get soggy.

---

4 10-ounce russet potatoes, rinsed, dried

½ cup milk

1 cup (packed) shredded Mexican-blend cheeses or grated cheddar cheese (about 4 ounces)

⅓ cup crushed nacho-flavored tortilla chips

⅓ cup chopped fresh cilantro

¼ cup chopped green onions

Sour cream

Salsa

Position rack in top third of oven and preheat to 425°F. Pierce each potato several times with toothpick or fork. Bake on rack until tender, about 1 hour 10 minutes (or microwave on high until tender, turning once, 10 to 15 minutes). Transfer potatoes to work surface. Maintain oven temperature.

Cut off top ¼ of 1 long side of each potato. Scoop potato flesh from skins into large bowl, leaving ¼-inch-thick shell. Mash potato flesh with milk. Mix in cheese, chips, cilantro and onions. Season with salt and pepper. Fill shells with potato mixture, mounding in center. (*Can be prepared 2 hours ahead. Cover with plastic and let stand at room temperature.*)

Return stuffed potatoes to oven and bake until heated through, about 20 minutes. Top potatoes with sour cream and salsa and then serve.

Baked Potatoes with Spinach and Cheese

This meatless main course gets a real flavor boost from Parmesan; yogurt lends tanginess.

VARIATION: Arugula would work in place of spinach.
DO-AHEAD: Make these up to two days ahead of time; rewarm just before serving.

4 SERVINGS

4 large russet potatoes, rinsed, dried	¼ cup plain yogurt
	¼ cup milk
2 teaspoons olive oil	½ cup freshly grated Parmesan cheese
6 garlic cloves, finely chopped	
1 10-ounce package ready-to-use spinach, stems trimmed	

Preheat oven to 400°F. Pierce potatoes several times with toothpick or fork. Bake potatoes until tender, about 1 hour (or microwave on high until tender, turning once, 10 to 15 minutes). Cool potatoes slightly. Cut potatoes in half lengthwise. Using spoon, scoop out potato flesh, leaving ¼-inch-thick shell. Place potato flesh in bowl and mash lightly. Arrange potato shells on baking sheet.

Heat oil in large nonstick skillet over medium heat. Add garlic and stir 30 seconds. Add spinach; cook just until wilted, about 2 minutes. Remove from heat. Add mashed potatoes, yogurt and milk and stir until blended. Season with salt and pepper. Spoon potato mixture into potato shells, dividing equally and mounding mixture slightly. Sprinkle grated Parmesan cheese over each potato. *(Can be prepared 2 days ahead. Cover and refrigerate.)*

Preheat oven to 350°F. Bake stuffed potatoes until tops are golden and potatoes are heated through, about 25 minutes. Serve immediately.

Twice-baked Potatoes
with Blue Cheese and Rosemary

Prepare a full recipe of these baked potatoes even if you only need a few servings; they keep well and would make a special treat for lunch at work (just microwave).

VARIATION: For a tangy, mellow flavor, try soft fresh goat cheese in place of the blue cheese.
DO-AHEAD: Note that these potatoes keep for two days in the refrigerator.

---

6 10-ounce russet potatoes, rinsed, dried

¼ cup plus 6 tablespoons sour cream

¼ cup (packed) plus 6 teaspoons crumbled
   blue cheese

¼ cup (½ stick) butter, room temperature

2 garlic cloves, minced

1½ teaspoons chopped fresh rosemary

6 SERVINGS

Preheat oven to 400°F. Pierce potatoes several times with toothpick or fork. Place potatoes on oven rack and bake until cooked through, about 1 hour 15 minutes (or microwave on high until tender, turning once, 10 to 15 minutes). Transfer to baking sheet; cool 5 minutes. Cut off top third of each potato. Using spoon, scoop potato flesh from bottoms into bowl, leaving ¼-inch-thick shell. Scoop potato flesh from tops, add to bowl. Discard tops.

Add ¼ cup sour cream, ¼ cup blue cheese, butter, garlic and rosemary to potato flesh; mash. Season with salt and pepper. Transfer mixture to pastry bag fitted with large star tip; pipe into potato shells, dividing equally. *(Can be prepared 2 days ahead. Cover and chill.)*

Preheat oven to 400°F. Place potatoes on baking sheet and bake until heated through and tops are beginning to brown, about 25 minutes. Spoon 1 tablespoon sour cream atop each potato. Sprinkle 1 teaspoon crumbled blue cheese over each potato and serve.

Potatoes Stuffed
with Cheddar Cheese and Bacon

For a complete meal, serve these potatoes with a spinach salad.

VARIATION: Many cheese and meat combinations would work well in place of the cheddar and bacon here; try Fontina and smoked sausage, Havarti and pancetta or Gouda and prosciutto—or a combination of your own.

DO-AHEAD: Prepare the potatoes up to two days ahead.

4 SERVINGS

4 large russet potatoes, rinsed, dried

½ cup chopped green onions

4 bacon slices, cooked, chopped

½ cup grated sharp cheddar cheese
(about 2 ounces)

½ cup sour cream

2 tablespoons (¼ stick) butter

Preheat oven to 375°F. Pierce potatoes several times with toothpick or fork. Bake potatoes until cooked through, about 1 hour 10 minutes (or microwave on high until tender, turning once, 10 to 15 minutes). Remove potatoes from oven; let cool 5 minutes. Maintain oven temperature.

Slice ½ inch off top of potatoes and set aside. Scoop out potato flesh from skins into large bowl, leaving ¼-inch-thick shell. Using fork, mash potato flesh. Coarsely chop reserved potato-skin tops and add to bowl with mashed potato. Add green onions, bacon, cheese and sour cream and mix well. Season potato mixture to taste with salt and pepper. Spoon mixture into potato shells, dividing equally. Dot each potato with ½ tablespoon butter. *(Can be prepared 2 days ahead. Cover and refrigerate.)*

Place stuffed potatoes on rimmed baking sheet. Bake until tops brown slightly and potatoes are heated through, about 30 minutes. Serve immediately.

Baked Potatoes with Spiced Beef Chili

Serve these with a green salad with olives and roasted red peppers.

VARIATION: The chili works over French fries for that fast-food classic—chili fries.
DO-AHEAD: Note that the chili can be made ahead of time.

4 SERVINGS

1 pound lean ground beef

2 tablespoons chili powder

1½ tablespoons dried oregano

1 teaspoon ground cinnamon

2 14½-ounce cans stewed tomatoes

1½ tablespoons red wine vinegar

4 8-ounce Yukon Gold potatoes, rinsed, dried

Sauté beef in heavy large skillet over medium-high heat 4 minutes, breaking up meat with back of fork. Mix in chili powder, oregano and cinnamon. Add tomatoes and bring to simmer, breaking up large tomato pieces with fork. Reduce heat, cover and simmer 8 minutes to blend flavors. Uncover and simmer until chili thickens slightly, stirring often, about 3 minutes. Add vinegar; season chili to taste with salt and pepper. *(Can be prepared 2 days ahead. Cover and refrigerate. Bring to simmer or rewarm in microwave before continuing.)*

Preheat oven to 400°F. Pierce potatoes several times with toothpick or fork. Place potatoes on oven rack and bake until cooked though, about 1 hour 15 minutes (or microwave on high until tender, turning once, about 10 to 15 minutes).

Split baked potatoes lengthwise; fluff insides lightly with fork. Place 2 potato halves on each plate. Ladle chili over potatoes and then serve immediately.

Sweet Potatoes Topped with Vegetarian Black Bean Chili

This one-dish meal is satisfying and hearty. Serve with frosty mugs of beer.

VARIATION: Top with sour cream instead of yogurt for a richer version of this entrée.
DO-AHEAD: Note that the chili can be prepared a day ahead.

4 SERVINGS

4 large tan-skinned sweet potatoes, rinsed, dried

1 tablespoon olive oil

2 cups diced red bell peppers

1½ cups chopped onions

3 garlic cloves, minced

1 tablespoon chili powder

2 teaspoons ground cumin

1 14½- to 16-ounce can peeled tomatoes in juice

1 15- to 16-ounce can black beans, rinsed thoroughly, drained

2 cups diced yellow crookneck squash

1 tablespoon minced seeded jalapeño chili

4 lime wedges

Plain yogurt (optional)

Chopped fresh cilantro (optional)

Preheat oven to 400°F. Place sweet potatoes in baking dish. Pierce sweet potatoes several times with toothpick or fork and bake until tender, about 1 hour 15 minutes (or microwave potatoes on high until tender, turning once, about 10 to 15 minutes).

Meanwhile, heat oil in large nonstick skillet over medium-low heat. Add bell peppers and onions and sauté until golden brown, about 10 minutes. Add garlic and stir 2 minutes. Stir in chili powder and cumin, then tomatoes with juices and beans. Bring mixture to simmer. Reduce heat to low, cover and cook 20 minutes. *(Sweet potatoes and chili can be prepared 1 day ahead. Cover separately and refrigerate. Rewarm potatoes in oven and chili over low heat before continuing.)* Add squash and jalapeño to chili; cover and cook until squash is crisp-tender, about 6 minutes.

Arrange 1 sweet potato on each plate. Split potatoes open; fluff insides lightly with fork. Spoon some chili into center of each. Squeeze lime juice over. Top with yogurt and chopped cilantro, if desired. Serve, passing remaining chili separately.

Turkey Sloppy Joe Baked Potatoes

Ground turkey, green chilies and ale make for an updated version of sloppy joes—and a great topping for baked potatoes.

VARIATION: Prepare this with ground beef for a more classic version of sloppy joes.
DO-AHEAD: The turkey topping can be prepared two days ahead.

---

3 tablespoons olive oil

1½ pounds ground turkey

1 large green bell pepper, chopped

4 large garlic cloves, chopped

3 tablespoons chili powder

1¼ cups ale or beer

¾ cup bottled chili sauce or ketchup

1 4-ounce can diced green chilies

2 tablespoons Worcestershire sauce

1 cup finely chopped green onions

6 10-ounce russet potatoes, rinsed, dried

Heat oil in heavy large pot over medium-high heat. Add turkey, bell pepper and garlic and sauté until turkey is no longer pink, breaking up meat with back of fork, about 10 minutes. Mix in chili powder; stir 1 minute. Add next 4 ingredients. Reduce heat to medium-low and simmer until mixture thickens, stirring often, about 15 minutes. *(Can be prepared 2 days ahead. Cover and refrigerate. Bring to simmer over medium heat before continuing.)* Mix in green onions; season with salt and pepper.

Preheat oven to 400°F. Pierce potatoes several times with toothpick or fork. Bake potatoes until tender, about 1 hour (or microwave on high until tender, turning once, 10 to 15 minutes). Place 1 potato on each plate. Split potatoes open; fluff insides lightly with fork. Spoon some sauce into each potato, dividing equally, and then serve.

Goat Cheese, Chive and Onion Baked Potatoes

Tangy goat cheese makes a great baked potato topping when mixed with chopped red onion, cream and fresh chives.

VARIATION: Try using cream cheese instead of goat cheese for a milder version of this recipe. Green onions can stand in for chives.

DO-AHEAD: Note that the topping can be prepared ahead of time.

---

6 SERVINGS

2 5.5-ounce logs soft fresh goat cheese (such as Montrachet)

1 small red onion, finely chopped

1 cup whipping cream

1 bunch of fresh chives, minced (about ½ cup)

6 10-ounce russet potatoes, rinsed, dried

Stir first 4 ingredients in medium bowl to blend. Season to taste with salt and pepper. *(Can be prepared up to 1 day ahead. Cover and refrigerate.)*

Preheat oven to 400°F. Pierce potatoes several times with toothpick or fork. Bake potatoes until tender, about 1 hour 10 minutes (or microwave on high until tender, turning once, 10 to 15 minutes). Place 1 potato on each plate. Split potatoes open; fluff insides lightly with fork. Add ¼ cup goat cheese mixture to each potato; mash into potato flesh with fork. Season with salt and pepper. Top each potato with another ¼ cup goat cheese mixture and serve.

Pesto-Broccoli Baked Potatoes

Purchased pesto and broccoli are combined to make this deliciously simple potato topping.

VARIATION: Try using walnuts instead of pine nuts, and Romano in place of Parmesan.

4 10-ounce russet potatoes, rinsed, dried

4 cups broccoli florets
1 7-ounce package purchased pesto
¼ cup pine nuts, toasted
¼ cup grated Parmesan cheese

Preheat oven to 400°F. Pierce potatoes several times with toothpick or fork. Bake until tender, about 1 hour 10 minutes (or microwave on high until tender, turning once, 10 to 15 minutes).

Meanwhile, steam broccoli florets until crisp-tender, about 6 minutes. Transfer to medium bowl; add all but 4 tablespoons pesto and stir to coat. Place 1 potato on each of 4 plates. Split potatoes open; fluff insides lightly with fork. Add 1 tablespoon reserved pesto to each potato; mash into potato flesh with fork. Top potatoes with pesto-broccoli mixture, dividing equally. Sprinkle each potato with pine nuts and Parmesan cheese, dividing equally, and serve.

POTATOES PLUS

Few suppers are as simple as a baked potato. Add a quick and easy-to-make topping and that meal goes from simple to super. Here are several fast topping ideas.

- Grated Parmesan, olive oil and coarsely cracked black pepper.
- Black beans seasoned with cumin and mixed with salsa and grated Monterey Jack cheese.
- Browned Italian sausages mixed with tomato sauce and grated Fontina or Parmesan cheese.
- Cottage cheese, chopped fresh tomatoes or green onions and coarsely cracked black pepper.
- Fresh or frozen spinach sautéed with curry powder and mixed with plain yogurt.

Pizzas Better Than Delivered

A delivered pizza is fast, but a homemade pizza is delicious. These recipes are both—fast because they make use of ready-made crusts, and delicious because they combine toppings in new and clever ways.

Three-Cheese Spinach Calzones

A calzone is a stuffed pizza; serve this one with black and green olives and grilled or roasted vegetables tossed with olive oil. Strawberries served with mascarpone cheese would be a simple yet unexpected dessert.

VARIATION: Substitute sautéed mushrooms and broccoli florets for the spinach, and grated Swiss cheese for the Fontina to make a different kind of calzone.

DO-AHEAD: The filling can be made ahead. Bake the calzones just before serving.

---

2 10-ounce packages frozen chopped spinach, thawed, squeezed dry

6 green onions, chopped

1 cup part-skim ricotta cheese

1 cup crumbled Gorgonzola or blue cheese (about 4 ounces)

2 cups (packed) grated Fontina cheese (about 8 ounces)

All purpose flour

2 10-ounce tubes refrigerated pizza dough

4 SERVINGS

Preheat oven to 425°F. Mix spinach, green onions, ricotta, Gorgonzola and then Fontina in medium bowl to blend. Season with salt and pepper. *(Can be made 6 hours ahead. Cover and refrigerate.)*

Sprinkle 2 heavy large baking sheets with flour. Unfold dough on prepared sheets. Gently stretch and/or roll dough to 11-inch squares; cut each in half diagonally, forming 4 triangles total. Place ¼ of filling in center of each triangle. Fold 1 side of each triangle over filling, forming 4 triangular calzones. Press edges of dough to seal. Cut 3 slits in top of each to allow steam to escape.

Bake calzones until golden brown, about 15 minutes; serve hot.

Grilled Pizzas Provençale

Marinated bell peppers, mushrooms and eggplant would be fine accompaniments to these grilled Mediterranean-style pizzas.

VARIATION: Coarsely chopped marinated artichoke hearts or chopped sautéed eggplant would also make great toppings for the pizzas.

DO-AHEAD: Prepare the toppings ahead of time, leaving only the grilling to do.

4 SERVINGS

3 cups chopped seeded plum tomatoes
(about 6 large)

2 cups chopped arugula

24 Kalamata olives or other brine-cured black
olives, pitted, halved

2 tablespoons olive oil

4 garlic cloves, chopped

All purpose flour

2 10-ounce tubes refrigerated pizza dough

2 cups crumbled soft fresh goat cheese
(such as Montrachet; about 5 ounces)

Stir tomatoes, arugula, olives, oil and garlic in medium bowl to combine; season topping with salt and pepper. *(Can be prepared 4 hours ahead. Cover and refrigerate.)*

Prepare barbecue (medium heat). Sprinkle 2 heavy large baking sheets with flour. Unfold pizza dough on prepared baking sheets; cut each dough piece into 4 pieces (each about 5x5 inches). Transfer dough, floured side down, to barbecue. Grill until bottoms are golden, about 5 minutes. Using spatula, return dough, grilled side up, to same baking sheets. Brush off any excess flour. Divide tomato topping and then goat cheese among crusts.

Using spatula, transfer pizzas to grill. Cover with grill top or heavy-duty foil. Grill until bottoms are brown and topping is heated through, about 3 minutes. Serve pizzas hot.

Prosciutto, Mozzarella and Basil Pizzas

The classic combination of tomatoes, basil and mozzarella cheese is unbeatable, especially with the addition of prosciutto. Serve these pizza squares with a simple radicchio and romaine salad dressed with balsamic vinaigrette.

VARIATION: For a vegetarian version, omit the prosciutto and sprinkle half a cup of freshly grated Parmesan cheese over the pizza before baking for a flavor boost.

4 SERVINGS

All purpose flour

2 10-ounce tubes refrigerated pizza dough

2 14½-ounce cans seasoned pasta-style tomatoes, well drained

1 cup thinly sliced prosciutto

⅔ cup thinly sliced fresh basil or

    2 tablespoons dried

2 cups (packed) grated mozzarella cheese
    (about 8 ounces)

Preheat oven to 425°F. Lightly sprinkle 2 heavy large baking sheets with flour. Unfold dough on prepared baking sheets. Stretch and/or roll dough to two 9x12-inch rectangles. Sprinkle tomatoes, then prosciutto and basil over dough, leaving 1-inch border. Top with cheese.

Bake pizzas until cheese melts and crust is golden brown, about 12 minutes. Transfer pizzas to work surface. Cut into squares and serve hot.

PIZZA AS YOU LIKE IT

With ready-made doughs on hand (and these include everything from frozen bread dough to a baked pizza crust, refrigerated pizza dough to a boxed mix), homemade pizza really can be faster than the delivered kind. And you can make it just the way you like it—ideal for finicky eaters like kids. Here are some quick topping combos to try. Mix and match to your heart's content.

- Caramelized onions.
- Lightly sautéed arugula, watercress or radicchio.
- Marinated artichoke hearts, drained and coarsely chopped.
- Marinated mushrooms, drained and coarsely chopped.
- Sliced brine-cured black olives.
- Chopped sun-dried tomatoes.
- Lightly sautéed strips of prosciutto or ham.
- Crumbled cooked bacon and sausage.
- Goat cheese or Monterey Jack (instead of mozzarella).
- Purchased pesto (spread over the crust in a thin layer).
- Chopped fresh herbs (chives with seafood pizza; thyme, oregano and basil with just about any kind of pizza).

Double-crusted Turkey Sausage Pizzas

You can dress up canned or frozen bean soup with chopped fresh sage and diced tomatoes to serve with these Sicilian-style pizzas.

VARIATION: Any Italian sausage can be used in place of the turkey sausage.

4 SERVINGS

1 pound Italian hot turkey sausages, casings removed

1 cup plus 6 tablespoons (packed) grated mozzarella cheese

1 cup coarsely chopped drained roasted red peppers from jar

6 tablespoons purchased pesto

All purpose flour

2 10-ounce tubes refrigerated pizza dough

Preheat oven to 450°F. Sauté sausages in heavy large skillet over medium-high heat until cooked through, breaking into small pieces with back of spoon, about 5 minutes. Using slotted spoon, transfer sausage to bowl. Mix in 1 cup cheese, red peppers and pesto; season with salt and pepper.

Lightly sprinkle 2 heavy large baking sheets with flour. Unfold dough on prepared sheets; cut dough in half crosswise. Stretch and/or roll each dough half into thin rectangle, approximately 7x10 inches. Press half of sausage mixture atop 1 dough rectangle, leaving generous ½-inch border. Top with another dough rectangle. Roll edges of dough together and press with fork to seal. Cut several slits in top to allow steam to escape. Repeat with remaining sausage mixture and dough rectangles. *(Can be prepared 2 hours ahead. Cover and refrigerate.)*

Bake pizzas until crust is pale golden, about 10 minutes. Sprinkle each with 3 tablespoons cheese. Bake until cheese melts, about 3 minutes longer. Serve hot.

Pizza with Roasted Garlic, Onion and Bell Peppers

An entire head of garlic is roasted, then pureed with sun-dried tomatoes for the delicious garlic paste that is spread over a purchased baked pizza crust.

VARIATION: Use Gorgonzola cheese in place of feta for a different taste.

DO-AHEAD: Note that the garlic paste and the roasted onions can be made ahead of time.

---

1 large head of garlic, unpeeled

2 tablespoons olive oil

1 large red or yellow onion, cut into
½-inch-thick slices

⅓ cup oil-packed sun-dried tomatoes, drained,
oil reserved

1 10-ounce purchased fully baked thin pizza crust

2 cups grated mozzarella cheese (about 6 ounces)

½ cup drained roasted red peppers from a jar,
cut into ½-inch-thick strips

⅔ cup (about 2½ ounces) crumbled feta cheese

4 tablespoons chopped fresh basil or
1 tablespoon dried

2 tablespoons chopped fresh parsley

4 SERVINGS

Preheat oven to 375°F. Slice top off garlic head; place in small baking dish. Drizzle with 1 tablespoon oil. Brush baking sheet with ½ tablespoon oil. Place onion slices on sheet and brush slices with ½ tablespoon oil. Bake garlic and onion until garlic cloves are light brown and soft and onion is tender, about 45 minutes. Remove from oven; let cool.

Using fingers, squeeze out roasted garlic cloves into food processor; add sun-dried tomatoes. Using on/off turns, process until almost smooth, adding enough reserved oil from sun-dried tomatoes to form paste. *(Onions and garlic paste can be prepared 1 day ahead. Cover separately; chill.)*

Preheat oven to 450°F. Place crust on baking sheet or pizza pan. Spread garlic paste evenly over crust. Top with mozzarella cheese, roasted onion, pepper strips and feta cheese. Sprinkle with 2 tablespoons basil and 1 tablespoon parsley. Bake pizza until crust is golden brown and cheese bubbles, about 8 minutes. Transfer to cutting board. Cool 5 minutes. Sprinkle with remaining 2 tablespoons basil and 1 tablespoon parsley. Cut into wedges and serve hot.

Quick Kielbasa Pizzas
with Zucchini and Mushrooms

Purchased pre-baked crusts make an effortless base for these pizzas.

VARIATION: Substitute 20 thin pepperoni slices for the sausage, adding 5 pepperoni slices to each pizza atop the vegetable mixture. Sprinkle with cheese and bake.

¼ cup olive oil

2 small zucchini, diced

1½ cups diced kielbasa sausage (about ½ pound)

8 mushrooms, sliced

½ cup chopped drained oil-packed
   sun-dried tomatoes

2 tablespoons chopped fresh basil or
   2 teaspoons dried

2 tablespoons chopped fresh oregano or
   2 teaspoons dried

4 6-inch purchased fully baked pizza crusts
   (from two 8-ounce packages)

8 tablespoons purchased pizza sauce

8 tablespoons grated Parmesan cheese

8 tablespoons grated mozzarella cheese

4 ounces goat cheese, crumbled

Heat oil in heavy large skillet over medium-low heat. Add zucchini, sausage and mushrooms and sauté until vegetables are almost tender, about 5 minutes. Add sun-dried tomatoes and sauté until vegetables are tender, about 3 minutes longer. Remove skillet from heat; stir in basil and oregano. *(Can be prepared 1 day ahead. Cover and refrigerate.)*

Preheat oven to 450°F. Arrange pizza crusts on large baking sheet. Spread 2 tablespoons pizza sauce over each. Sprinkle each with 2 tablespoons Parmesan. Divide vegetable mixture among pizzas. Top each with 2 tablespoons mozzarella and ¼ of goat cheese. Bake until mozzarella melts and pizzas are heated through, about 9 minutes. Serve hot.

Garlic-Pancetta Pizzas

Serve with a mixed green salad from the salad bar and a glass of Chianti.

VARIATION: For an easier version, replace the rosemary tomatoes with two 14½-ounce cans of diced tomatoes with Italian seasonings (drained), stirring in 1 tablespoon minced rosemary. DO-AHEAD: Note that the rosemary tomatoes can be prepared ahead of time.

ROSEMARY TOMATOES

2 16-ounce cans Italian plum tomatoes, drained, chopped

⅓ cup olive oil

3 green onions, chopped

2 garlic cloves, minced

2 tablespoons red wine vinegar

1 tablespoon minced fresh rosemary or 1 teaspoon dried

Pinch of dried crushed red pepper

PIZZAS

½ pound ¼-inch-thick pancetta* or smoked bacon slices

8 garlic cloves, minced

2 16-ounce purchased fully baked pizza crusts

2 cups (packed) grated mozzarella cheese (about 8 ounces)

½ cup sliced drained oil-packed sun-dried tomatoes

2 tablespoons chopped fresh basil or 2 teaspoons dried

1 tablespoon chopped fresh sage or 1 teaspoon dried rubbed sage

8 SERVINGS

FOR ROSEMARY TOMATOES: Mix all ingredients in large bowl. Cover and refrigerate overnight. *(Can be prepared 4 days ahead. Keep refrigerated. Drain before using.)*

FOR PIZZAS: Preheat oven to 500°F. Cook pancetta in heavy large skillet over medium heat until brown and crisp. Using tongs, transfer pancetta to paper towels and drain. Chop pancetta. Pour off all but 1 tablespoon drippings from skillet. Add garlic and sauté over low heat until pale golden, about 5 minutes. Remove from heat. Place pizza crusts on 2 baking sheets. Sprinkle ½ cup mozzarella cheese over each crust. Sprinkle half of garlic over each. Top with rosemary tomatoes, dividing equally. Sprinkle sun-dried tomatoes, basil, sage, then pancetta over, dividing equally. Top each with ½ cup cheese. Bake until pizza crusts are crisp, about 15 minutes. Cut into wedges.

*Pancetta, Italian bacon cured in salt, is available at Italian markets and some specialty foods stores.

Cabbage, Bacon and Cheese Calzones

Frozen bread dough cuts down on the preparation time for these calzones.

VARIATION: Use sliced radicchio or drained thawed frozen spinach in place of cabbage.
DO-AHEAD: Note that the filling can be prepared a day ahead.

4 SERVINGS

4 slices thick-cut bacon, thinly sliced

½ medium onion, thinly sliced

¼ small cabbage, thinly sliced

⅛ teaspoon dried crushed red pepper

1 tablespoon balsamic vinegar

¼ teaspoon dried thyme

1½ cups grated mozzarella cheese (about 6 ounces)

1 cup grated Fontina cheese (about 3 ounces)

Olive oil

Additional dried crushed red pepper

Additional dried thyme

1½ pounds frozen bread dough, thawed

1 large egg yolk beaten with 1 tablespoon water

Preheat oven to 450°F. Sauté bacon in heavy large skillet over medium heat until cooked through, stirring frequently, about 3 minutes. Add onion, cabbage and ⅛ teaspoon dried red pepper and cook until cabbage is tender, stirring occasionally, about 12 minutes. Add vinegar and ¼ teaspoon thyme; season with salt and pepper. Cool. *(Can be prepared 1 day ahead. Cover and refrigerate.)*

Knead dough until smooth. Divide into 2 pieces. Roll 1 piece out on lightly floured surface to 11-inch round. Brush half of edge with yolk mixture. Spread half of mozzarella over half of dough without covering egg. Top with half of Fontina, then half of cabbage mixture. Fold other half of dough over. Press edges together with fork to seal. Trim edges. Transfer to baking sheet. Repeat with remaining dough, yolk mixture, cheeses and cabbage mixture.

Brush calzones with olive oil. Sprinkle with pepper and dried red pepper. Bake until golden brown, about 13 minutes. Brush with oil again; sprinkle with thyme. Serve immediately.

Broccoli, Pepperoni and Gorgonzola Pizza

Serve with a salad of romaine, walnuts and cherry tomatoes in a red wine vinaigrette.

VARIATION: Substitute two cups chopped broccoli *rabe* for the broccoli florets.
DO-AHEAD: The tomato sauce and steamed broccoli can be prepared ahead; the pizza should be put together and baked just before serving.

---

1 tablespoon butter

2 large garlic cloves, minced

1 cup canned crushed tomatoes with puree

2 teaspoons minced fresh oregano or
  ¾ teaspoon dried

2 cups broccoli florets

1 pound frozen bread dough, thawed
  Olive oil

2½ ounces pepperoni, thinly sliced

5 ounces Gorgonzola cheese, crumbled

Melt butter in heavy medium saucepan over medium-low heat. Add garlic and stir 2 minutes. Add tomatoes with puree. Increase heat and boil until sauce thickens, stirring frequently, about 6 minutes. Stir in oregano. Season sauce with pepper. Cool.

Cook broccoli in large pot of boiling salted water until just crisp-tender. Drain. Run under cold water to cool. Drain well. *(Can be prepared 1 day ahead; chill broccoli and sauce separately.)*

Position rack in top third of oven and preheat to 425°F. Lightly oil 13-inch pizza pan or baking sheet. Knead dough until smooth, about 1 minute. Cover and let rest 5 minutes. Roll out on lightly floured surface to 13-inch round. Transfer to prepared pan. Press to build up rim. Brush with oil. Bake 2 minutes to warm dough. Press to fit pan again. Spread tomato sauce over. Distribute pepperoni and broccoli over sauce. Top with cheese. Sprinkle with pepper. Bake until crust is brown and cheese bubbles, 15 to 20 minutes. Let stand 5 minutes before serving.

Meatless Night

Eating a vegetarian meal once or twice a week is a good thing, as we all know. But how to make that meal hearty and satisfying, tasty enough that we don't miss the meat? Here are nine great-tasting answers to that question.

Broiled Herbed Polenta
with Wild Mushrooms

Prepared polenta rolls are a popular new convenience item; look for them in the pasta section of your supermarket. Serve this entrée with a salad of radicchio, endive, marinated artichoke hearts, cherry tomatoes and Gorgonzola.

DO-AHEAD: Note that the mushroom sauté can be prepared up to one hour ahead.

---

3 tablespoons olive oil

1 pound fresh wild mushrooms (such as crimini, portobello, oyster or stemmed shiitake) and button mushrooms, sliced

4 garlic cloves, minced

⅔ cup canned vegetable broth

¼ cup dry Marsala or white wine

2 green onions, chopped

12 ½-inch-thick slices seasoned prepared polenta (from two 1- to 1½-pound rolls)

4 SERVINGS

Heat 2 tablespoons oil in heavy large skillet over medium heat. Add mushrooms and garlic and sauté until mushrooms soften, about 6 minutes. Add broth, Marsala and green onions and simmer until liquid is reduced by half, scraping up browned bits, about 5 minutes. Season to taste with salt and pepper. *(Can be prepared 1 hour ahead. Cover and let stand at room temperature. Stir over medium heat to heat through before continuing.)*

Preheat broiler. Arrange polenta slices on large baking sheet. Brush polenta on both sides with remaining 1 tablespoon oil. Broil polenta until golden and crisp, about 3 minutes per side.

Transfer polenta to plates. Spoon mushrooms and sauce over and serve.

Spinach Soufflé
with Roasted Red Pepper Sauce

Serve with a Bibb lettuce and endive salad with walnut oil vinaigrette and French bread.

2 TO 4 SERVINGS

1 10-ounce package frozen creamed spinach, thawed

¾ cup coarsely grated Swiss or Jarlsberg cheese (about 3 ounces)

¼ teaspoon salt

¼ teasoon ground black pepper

2 large egg yolks

3 large egg whites

1 7.25-ounce jar roasted red peppers, drained well, 1 tablespoon juices reserved

1 teaspoon balsamic vinegar

1 large shallot, coarsely chopped

Preheat oven to 400°F. Butter 9-inch-diameter glass pie dish. Mix creamed spinach, grated Swiss cheese, salt and pepper in medium bowl; whisk in egg yolks. Using electric mixer, beat egg whites in large bowl until stiff but not dry; fold into spinach mixture. Gently transfer to prepared dish.

Bake soufflé until beginning to color at edges and center is puffed and softly set, about 18 minutes.

Meanwhile, puree half of roasted red peppers, 1 tablespoon reserved red pepper juices and balsamic vinegar in processor until almost smooth. Add remaining roasted red peppers and shallot and chop, using on/off turns, to form chunky puree. Transfer sauce to small saucepan. Stir over medium heat until warmed through; season to taste with salt and pepper.

Spoon soufflé onto plates. Serve immediately, passing sauce separately.

Spicy Tofu Burritos

Tofu has a custard-like texture and is available in soft, firm and extra-firm varieties; firm is preferable here. Serve these topped with purchased salsa and plain nonfat yogurt.

VARIATION: Use pepper Jack instead of mozzarella to give these burritos even more heat.

---

4 7- to 8-inch-diameter flour tortillas

1 tablespoon olive oil

½ cup chopped onion

1½ teaspoons ground cumin

½ teaspoon turmeric

12 ounces firm tofu, crumbled (about 2 cups)

1 cup chopped red bell pepper

1½ tablespoons minced seeded jalapeño chili

1 garlic clove, minced

¾ cup grated mozzarella cheese (about 3 ounces)

1 cup (packed) thinly sliced romaine lettuce

6 tablespoons chopped fresh cilantro

4 lime wedges

4 SERVINGS

Preheat oven to 350°F. Wrap tortillas in foil. Place in oven until heated through, about 15 minutes.

Meanwhile, heat oil in large nonstick skillet over medium-high heat. Add onion and sauté until golden, about 5 minutes. Add cumin and turmeric; stir 30 seconds. Add tofu, bell pepper, jalapeño and garlic and sauté until heated through, about 3 minutes. Add cheese and stir until melted, about 1 minute. Season mixture to taste with salt and pepper.

Spoon tofu mixture down center of each tortilla, dividing equally. Top with lettuce and cilantro. Squeeze juice from lime wedges over. Wrap tortilla around filling and serve.

Peas and Potatoes Masala

Masala is an Indian blend of spices; potatoes and tofu give the dish substance. Round out this meal with warm _naan_ or pita bread, basmati rice and plain yogurt.

DO-AHEAD: Prepare this main course up to a day ahead of time.

4 SERVINGS

¼ cup vegetable oil

2 medium onions, chopped

2 14½-ounce cans diced tomatoes in juice

2 6- to 7-ounce russet potatoes, peeled,
    cut into ½-inch cubes

1 tablespoon ground cumin

1 teaspoon ground allspice

12 ounces firm or extra-firm tofu, drained well,
    cut into ½-inch pieces

3 cups frozen peas, thawed

½ cup chopped fresh cilantro

Heat oil in heavy large skillet over medium heat. Add onions; sauté until golden, about 6 minutes. Add tomatoes with juices, potatoes, cumin and allspice. Cover; simmer until potatoes are just tender, stirring occasionally, about 8 minutes. Add tofu, peas and cilantro. Simmer uncovered until vegetables are tender, about 6 minutes. Season with salt and pepper. _(Can be prepared 1 day ahead. Cover and refrigerate. Bring to simmer over medium heat or reheat in microwave before serving.)_

West Indian Rice and Beans

This risotto-like dish is delicious served with fruit salad sprinkled with coconut.

4 SERVINGS

5 cups (about) canned vegetable broth

2 15- to 16-ounce cans kidney beans, drained

1 14-ounce can unsweetened regular or
   light coconut milk

2 tablespoons minced seeded jalapeño chilies

2 teaspoons dried thyme

½ teaspoon ground allspice

1½ cups medium-grain white rice

2 cups thinly sliced green onions

Combine 4 cups broth, beans, coconut milk, minced chilies, thyme and allspice in heavy large saucepan. Bring mixture to boil over medium-high heat. Stir in rice. Reduce heat to medium-low and simmer mixture, uncovered, until most of liquid is absorbed and rice is almost tender, stirring often, approximately 20 minutes.

Mix 1½ cups green onions into rice. Continue to simmer until rice is very tender and mixture is creamy, adding more broth by ½ cup-fuls if mixture seems dry, about 5 minutes longer. Season to taste with salt and pepper. Transfer to serving bowl. Sprinkle with remaining ½ cup green onions and serve.

THE VEGETARIAN KITCHEN

Once upon a time, a meatless meal meant mounds of cooked bulgur and buckwheat or a lackluster bean soup that may have been virtuous but did not make culinary memories. Now eating meatless is easier than ever, not to mention a lot tastier. Fill the pantry, fridge and freezer with these foods for meatless meals in a flash.

- Canned beans (*cannellini,* kidney, navy, black, garbanzo).
- Dried beans (lentils, garbanzo, black, navy, kidney, fava, cranberry, adzuki, flageolets, split peas, black-eyed peas, mung).
- Frozen beans (lima, black-eyed peas, green peas, *edamame*).
- Grains (polenta, kasha, bulgur, rice, pearl barley, millet, rolled oats, wheat berries).
- Couscous.
- Pasta (a variety of shapes and sizes).
- Breads (store in the freezer).
- Vegetable broth (canned, bouillon cubes or homemade).
- Eggs.
- Tofu.
- Tempeh (fermented soybean cake).
- Plain yogurt.
- Nuts (store in the freezer).

Goat Cheese and Green Onion Pan Soufflé

This easy soufflé mixes in minutes and bakes in a skillet. Have steamed artichokes to start; accompany the soufflé with a whole wheat baguette and sliced tomatoes.

2 TO 4 SERVINGS

3 large eggs, separated

⅓ cup (packed) soft fresh goat cheese
(such as Montrachet)

½ cup half and half

⅓ cup all purpose flour

½ teaspoon salt

¼ teaspoon pepper

3 tablespoons chopped green onions

1 tablespoon chopped fresh tarragon, basil or chives

1 tablespoon butter

Preheat oven to 400°F. Whisk yolks and cheese in medium bowl to blend. Whisk in half and half. Add flour, salt and pepper; whisk until smooth. Mix in green onions and tarragon. Beat whites in another medium bowl until stiff but not dry. Gently fold whites into cheese mixture in 2 additions.

Melt butter in heavy 9-inch ovenproof skillet (with about 4-cup capacity) over medium-high heat. Tilt skillet to coat evenly with butter. Pour soufflé mixture into hot skillet.

Bake soufflé until puffed and golden, about 20 minutes. Serve immediately.

Grilled Portobello and Arugula Burgers

Portobello mushrooms have a rich, hearty flavor that makes them a great replacement for the hamburger patty in these burgers.

VARIATION: Use red leaf lettuce in place of arugula, if you like. Add a slice of provolone or Swiss cheese to each burger for even more taste.

½ cup mayonnaise

2 teaspoons Dijon mustard

6 teaspoons minced fresh rosemary

1 garlic clove, minced

Nonstick vegetable oil spray

4 large portobello mushrooms, stems trimmed

2 tablespoons olive oil

4 whole wheat buns, toasted

2 cups arugula

4 SERVINGS

Whisk mayonnaise, mustard, 2 teaspoons rosemary and garlic in small bowl to blend. Set aside.

Spray grill rack with nonstick oil spray, then prepare barbecue (medium heat). Brush mushrooms all over with olive oil. Sprinkle each with 1 teaspoon minced fresh rosemary, then salt and pepper. Grill mushrooms until tender, about 10 minutes per side.

Spread mayonnaise mixture over buns. Place mushrooms and arugula on bun bottoms. Cover with bun tops. Serve burgers immediately.

Walnut Risotto with Roasted Asparagus

Adding sliced ripe tomatoes with basil would make this a complete meal.

VARIATION: Replace the walnuts with pine nuts and the asparagus with trimmed, quartered baby artichokes (they'll cook in about the same amount of time).

4 SERVINGS

4½ to 5 cups canned vegetable broth	1 pound asparagus, tough ends trimmed
4 teaspoons extra-virgin olive oil	1 large garlic clove, thinly sliced
⅓ cup chopped onion	
1¼ cups arborio rice or medium-grain white rice	¼ cup finely chopped toasted walnuts
½ cup dry white wine	¼ cup freshly grated Parmesan cheese

Preheat oven to 450°F. Bring broth to simmer in medium saucepan. Cover and remove from heat. Heat 2 teaspoons olive oil in heavy medium saucepan over medium-high heat. Add onion and sauté until light golden, about 4 minutes. Add rice and stir 1 minute. Add wine and stir until wine evaporates, about 2 minutes. Add ½ cup hot broth and cook until liquid is absorbed, stirring frequently. Continue adding broth, ½ cupful at a time, until rice is tender and creamy, stirring frequently and allowing most of broth to be absorbed before adding more, about 25 minutes.

Meanwhile, place asparagus and sliced garlic in shallow baking dish. Drizzle remaining 2 teaspoons oil over. Sprinkle with salt and pepper. Toss asparagus to coat with oil. Bake asparagus until tender, turning occasionally, approximately 16 minutes.

Mix walnuts and grated Parmesan into risotto. Season to taste with salt and pepper. Arrange roasted asparagus in center of 4 plates. Top with risotto and serve immediately.

Poblano Chilies Stuffed with Black Beans and Cheese

This baked version of the Mexican favorite, which is usually battered and fried, is served atop a bed of rich-tasting caramelized onions. Serve with warm tortillas.

VARIATION: Pinto beans could stand in for the black beans, and pepper Jack cheese could replace the regular Jack here to give this entrée an extra kick of flavor. For an even easier version, purchase two seven-ounce cans of whole green chilies, drain and use in place of fresh ones, omitting the steps of roasting, peeling and seeding.

DO-AHEAD: Prepare the stuffed chilies and sautéed onions up to four hours ahead; put them in the oven 20 minutes or so before dinner.

---

8 large poblano chilies*

1 tablespoon olive oil

3 cups thinly sliced onions

2 15- to 16-ounce cans black beans,
   rinsed, drained

¼ teaspoon cayenne pepper

2 cups grated Monterey Jack cheese
   (about 8 ounces)

Tomato salsa

Sour cream

8 SERVINGS

Preheat broiler. Arrange chilies on baking sheet. Broil until charred on all sides, turning occasionally, about 20 minutes. Enclose chilies in paper bag; let stand 10 minutes. Peel chilies. Cut 1 lengthwise slit in each chili; carefully remove seeds and discard.

Meanwhile, heat oil in large nonstick skillet over medium-low heat. Add onions; sauté until golden, about 20 minutes. Season with salt and pepper. Spread in 13x9x2-inch glass baking dish.

Preheat oven to 350°F. Mash half of beans with cayenne in medium bowl. Mix in remaining beans. Spoon mixture into chilies. Arrange chilies seam side down atop onions. Sprinkle cheese over. Cover with foil. *(Can be made 4 hours ahead. Cover and refrigerate.)*

Bake chilies 15 minutes. Uncover; bake until cheese melts, about 5 minutes longer. Serve immediately over caramelized onions; top with salsa and sour cream.

*Fresh green chilies, often called *pasillas;* available at Latin American markets and some supermarkets.

Good for You

Calories, fat and cholesterol—these are things we keep an eye on a good part of the time. But some nights you want to make sure your dinner is as lean and mean as it gets, guaranteed good for you, as it were. That's where these healthful recipes come in.

Beef Medallions with Jalapeño Relish

Tangy mashed potatoes made with a dollop of low-fat sour cream instead of butter would round out this satisfying meal perfectly.

VARIATION: The jalapeño relish would also be delicious served with pork chops.
DO-AHEAD: Note that the relish can be made ahead.

½ cup water

¼ cup sugar

1 tablespoon cider vinegar

6 large fresh jalapeño chilies, seeded, thinly sliced
(about 4 ounces)

¼ cup thinly sliced onion

1 teaspoon mustard seeds

¼ cup matchstick-size strips red bell pepper

¼ cup matchstick-size strips yellow bell pepper

¼ cup thinly sliced carrot

8 ⅓-inch-thick lean beef tenderloin slices
(about 2 ounces each)

2 teaspoons vegetable oil

Fresh cilantro sprigs (optional)

4 SERVINGS

Combine ½ cup water, sugar and vinegar in small saucepan and bring to boil. Add chilies, onion and mustard seeds and cook 3 minutes, stirring occasionally. Add bell peppers and carrot and stir 2 minutes. Cool. Cover and chill. *(Can be made 2 days ahead. Bring to room temperature before using.)*

Sprinkle beef slices with salt and pepper. Lightly brush large nonstick skillet with oil and heat over high heat. Add beef and cook until brown, about 1 minute per side. Arrange 2 beef slices on each of 4 plates; surround with small spoonfuls of relish. Garnish with cilantro sprigs.

PER SERVING: CALORIES, 276; TOTAL FAT, 11 G; SATURATED FAT, 3.5 G; CHOLESTEROL, 71 MG.

Roasted Salmon
with Orange-Herb Sauce

Serve with steamed fresh asparagus and rice pilaf. Toasted slices of angel food cake would make a deceptively light dessert.

VARIATION: This would also be great made with red snapper.

6 SERVINGS

1 large orange, unpeeled, sliced

1 large onion, halved, thinly sliced

1½ tablespoons olive oil

6 3-ounce skinless salmon fillets

3 tablespoons chopped fresh dill

½ cup orange juice

¼ cup thinly sliced green onions

1½ tablespoons fresh lemon juice

Additional unpeeled orange slices

Preheat oven to 400°F. Place orange slices in single layer in 13x9x2-inch glass baking dish. Top with onion slices. Drizzle with oil. Sprinkle with salt and pepper. Roast until onion is brown and tender, about 25 minutes. Remove from oven. Increase oven temperature to 450°F.

Push orange and onion slices to sides of baking dish. Arrange salmon in center of dish. Sprinkle with salt, pepper and 1½ tablespoons dill. Spoon orange and onion slices atop salmon. Roast until salmon is opaque in center, about 8 minutes.

Meanwhile, mix orange juice, green onions, lemon juice and remaining 1½ tablespoons dill in small bowl. Transfer salmon to platter. Spoon onion alongside; discard roasted orange slices. Pour orange sauce over fish. Garnish with additional orange slices.

PER SERVING: CALORIES, 196; TOTAL FAT, 10 G; SATURATED FAT, 1 G; CHOLESTEROL, 55 MG.

Sea Bass with Tomatoes and Green Beans

This one-dish main course needs only bread and wine to round out the meal.

VARIATION: Use halibut in place of the sea bass.

4 SERVINGS

1½ pounds plum tomatoes, each cut into 8 wedges

1 large onion, cut into wedges

2 garlic cloves, minced

1 tablespoon olive oil

8 ounces green beans, cut into 2-inch pieces

2 teaspoons curry powder

2 teaspoons minced peeled fresh ginger

4 5- to 6-ounce sea bass fillets

Preheat oven to 400°F. Mix tomatoes, onion and garlic on nonstick baking sheet. Drizzle with oil; toss to coat. Roast until onion begins to brown, stirring occasionally, about 35 minutes.

Remove baking sheet from oven; increase temperature to 450°F. Mix beans, curry and ginger into tomato mixture; top with fish. Sprinkle with salt and pepper. Spoon some tomato mixture over fish. Roast until fish is opaque in center, about 18 minutes. Serve.

PER SERVING: CALORIES, 261; TOTAL FAT, 7 G; SATURATED FAT, 1 G; CHOLESTEROL, 64 MG.

ADDING FLAVOR WITHOUT FAT

Cooking healthfully is less complicated than it can sometimes sound. It's really as simple as cooking with less fat. Keep this in mind, and you're on your way to a diet that's better for you. Here are some tips for keeping it healthy *and* tasty.

- Try a cast iron grill pan. The food rests on top of the pan's ridges and not in the oil, so it absorbs less.
- When poaching chicken, instead of using water, use a mixture of canned chicken broth and white wine. Add chopped carrots, onions and herbs for extra flavor.
- Grill or roast vegetables (cooking techniques that add flavor but not fat) instead of steaming or boiling them.
- Serve meats, fish and poultry with vegetable salsas instead of cream sauces or gravies.
- Seek out the best, freshest produce possible. The fresher it is, the less you have to add to it or do to it for great taste.

Provençal Lamb
with Mediterranean Vegetables

It takes just about 30 minutes to roast this elegant, healthful main course.

DO-AHEAD: Note that both the lamb and the vegetables can be prepared ahead of time. Roast the lamb and reheat the vegetables just before serving.

4 SERVINGS

2 teaspoons coriander seeds

2 teaspoons fennel seeds

2 teaspoons dried thyme

1 teaspoon salt

½ teaspoon ground black pepper

1 teaspoon olive oil

1 8-rib rack of lamb (about 1½ pounds), well trimmed

Mediterranean Vegetables (see recipe)

Coarsely grind first 3 ingredients in blender. Transfer to small bowl. Mix in salt and pepper. Rub oil, then spice mixture over lamb. Place on baking sheet; let stand 1 hour or cover and chill overnight.

Preheat oven to 425°F. Roast lamb until thermometer inserted into center of meat registers 130°F for medium-rare, about 25 minutes. Let stand 10 minutes. Cut lamb between ribs into chops. Place 2 chops on each plate. Spoon Mediterranean Vegetables alongside.

PER SERVING (WITHOUT VEGETABLES): CALORIES, 201; TOTAL FAT, 10 G; SATURATED FAT, 3 G; CHOLESTEROL, 81 MG.

Mediterranean Vegetables

4 SERVINGS

Nonstick vegetable oil spray

1 large red onion, cut into ¼-inch wedges

2 medium zucchini, sliced diagonally

2 yellow crookneck squash, sliced diagonally

2 tablespoons balsamic vinegar

1 tablespoon chopped fresh thyme

1 teaspoon olive oil

Preheat oven to 400°F. Spray large rimmed baking sheet with nonstick spray. Toss onion and next 5 ingredients together on prepared sheet; spread in single layer. Sprinkle with salt and pepper. Bake vegetables until tender and brown around edges, stirring occasionally, about 35 minutes. *(Can be prepared 1 day ahead. Cover and refrigerate. Reheat or serve at room temperature.)*

PER SERVING: CALORIES, 52; TOTAL FAT, 1 G; SATURATED FAT, 0.5 G; CHOLESTEROL, 0.

Seared Shrimp
with Warm New Potato Salad

This warm potato salad is made without mayonnaise—and you won't miss it.

VARIATION: Use fresh sea scallops instead of shrimp.

DO-AHEAD: Note that the shrimp can marinate up to two hours.

1 pound uncooked large shrimp, peeled, deveined

3 tablespoons extra-virgin olive oil

1 teaspoon minced fresh thyme or
   ½ teaspoon dried

1 teaspoon grated lemon peel

2 garlic cloves, pressed

2 pounds small red-skinned new potatoes,
   unpeeled, quartered

½ cup dry white wine

3 tablespoons fresh lemon juice

6 cups (packed) baby salad greens

1 cup quartered cherry tomatoes
   Lemon wedges

4 SERVINGS

Mix shrimp, 1 tablespoon oil, thyme, lemon peel and garlic in medium bowl. Sprinkle with salt and pepper. Let stand at room temperature 15 minutes or refrigerate up to 2 hours.

Cook potatoes in boiling salted water until just tender, about 15 minutes. Drain thoroughly. Transfer potatoes to bowl, cover and keep warm.

Meanwhile, heat large nonstick skillet over high heat. Add shrimp mixture and sauté just until shrimp are cooked through, about 4 minutes. Transfer shrimp to plate. Add wine to skillet and boil until reduced by half, about 1 minute. Remove from heat; add 1 tablespoon oil and 2 tablespoons lemon juice and stir to blend. Pour dressing over potatoes. Season with salt and pepper.

Mix greens, remaining 1 tablespoon oil and 1 tablespoon lemon juice in large bowl. Divide greens among 4 plates. Place potatoes in center of greens. Top with shrimp. Garnish with cherry tomatoes and lemon wedges and serve immediately.

PER SERVING: CALORIES, 487; TOTAL FAT, 13 G; SATURATED FAT, 2 G; CHOLESTEROL, 173 MG.

Chicken Packets
with Spinach and Cherry Tomatoes

Cooking the chicken in packets keeps it much more moist than ordinary baking but adds no fat the way sautéing or frying would. Serve with steamed new potatoes.

VARIATION: Swiss chard would work well instead of spinach in these packets; remove any tough stems before tearing it into pieces.

DO-AHEAD: The packets can be put together ahead of time. Bake just before serving.

4 SERVINGS

2 tablespoons minced fresh dill

2 teaspoons grated orange or lemon peel

1 garlic clove, minced

¾ teaspoon salt

1 cup cherry tomatoes, halved

1 tablespoon olive oil

4 skinless boneless chicken breast halves,
thinly sliced crosswise

4 cups (firmly packed) torn fresh spinach leaves
(about 8 ounces)

Mix dill, orange peel, garlic and salt in medium bowl. Season with pepper. Combine cherry tomatoes, oil and 1 teaspoon dill mixture in small bowl. Add sliced chicken to remaining dill mixture in medium bowl and then toss chicken to coat.

Cut 4 sheets of foil, each 20 inches long. Place 1 foil sheet on work surface. Arrange 1 cup spinach on 1 half of foil. Place ¼ of sliced chicken mixture atop spinach. Spoon ¼ of tomato mixture atop chicken. Fold foil over, enclosing contents completely and crimping edges tightly to seal. Repeat with remaining 3 foil sheets, spinach, chicken and tomato mixture, forming 4 packets. *(Can be prepared 4 hours ahead. Cover and refrigerate.)*

Preheat oven to 450°F. Place large baking sheet in oven to heat. Arrange foil packets in single layer on heated baking sheet. Reduce oven temperature to 400°F. Bake chicken until just cooked through, about 10 minutes. Transfer to plates; let stand 5 minutes.

PER SERVING: CALORIES, 241; TOTAL FAT, 8 G; SATURATED FAT, 2 G; CHOLESTEROL, 96 MG.

Breaded Chicken Cutlets
with Chunky Vegetable Sauce

Serve with sautéed fresh spinach and sourdough dinner rolls.

VARIATION: Use turkey cutlets instead, if you like. The chunky vegetable sauce in this recipe would also be good tossed with pasta and olive oil.

4 SERVINGS

4 large plum tomatoes, quartered

1 large onion, cut into ½-inch-wide wedges

2 red or green bell peppers, sliced

1 8-ounce zucchini, trimmed, halved lengthwise,
  sliced crosswise

1 tablespoon olive oil

Nonstick vegetable oil spray

1 cup dry breadcrumbs

4 large egg whites

4 skinless boneless chicken breast halves

¼ cup freshly grated Parmesan cheese

2 tablespoons chopped fresh Italian parsley

1 teaspoon chopped fresh thyme or
  ½ teaspoon dried

1 cup canned low-salt chicken broth, hot

Preheat oven to 400°F. Place vegetables on large rimmed baking sheet. Sprinkle with salt and pepper. Drizzle oil over; toss to coat. Roast vegetables until tender and brown around edges, turning occasionally, about 45 minutes. Remove from oven. Increase oven temperature to 500°F.

Meanwhile, spray large nonstick baking sheet with nonstick oil spray. Place breadcrumbs on sheet of waxed paper. Whisk egg whites in shallow bowl until foamy. Using mallet, pound chicken breasts to ⅓-inch thickness. Sprinkle chicken with salt and pepper. Turn chicken in breadcrumbs; place on platter. Stir Parmesan into remaining breadcrumbs on waxed paper. Dip chicken into egg whites to coat. Then dip chicken into Parmesan breadcrumbs to coat; shake off excess.

Transfer vegetables to bowl; mix in parsley and thyme. Add broth to rimmed baking sheet; scrape up any browned bits. Pour over vegetables. Keep warm.

Bake chicken on prepared sheet 5 minutes. Turn chicken over; bake just until cooked through, about 5 minutes longer. Transfer chicken to plates. Spoon vegetable sauce alongside.

PER SERVING: CALORIES, 333; TOTAL FAT, 10 G; SATURATED FAT, 3 G; CHOLESTEROL, 77 MG.

Braised Pork Cutlets
with Lemon-Thyme Sauce

A garlic-herb mixture adds lots of flavor without adding any fat to this entrée. Sautéed Swiss chard and butternut squash would make a colorful side dish.

VARIATION: This recipe would also be delicious prepared with veal cutlets.
DO-AHEAD: Note that the meat can marinate for up to one day.

4 SERVINGS

8 thin-cut boneless pork loin chops

3 tablespoons fresh lemon juice

1 tablespoon chopped fresh thyme or
   1 teaspoon dried

2 teaspoons grated lemon peel

2 garlic cloves, minced

1½ tablespoons all purpose flour

2 teaspoons olive oil

¾ cup low-fat (1%) milk

Place pork in 15x10x2-inch glass baking dish. Mix 2 tablespoons lemon juice, thyme, lemon peel and garlic in small bowl. Rub over both sides of chops. Cover; chill at least 1 hour and up to 1 day.

Transfer pork chops to baking sheet. Sprinkle each chop lightly with flour, then salt and pepper. Heat oil in large nonstick skillet over high heat. Working in batches, add pork to skillet and cook until brown, about 1 minute per side. Return all pork to skillet. Add milk and boil until pork is cooked through and sauce thickens slightly, about 1 minute. Transfer pork to platter. Whisk remaining 1 tablespoon lemon juice into sauce in skillet and stir to blend, 30 seconds. Season with salt and pepper. Pour sauce over pork and serve immediately.

PER SERVING: CALORIES, 193; TOTAL FAT, 7 G; SATURATED FAT, 2 G; CHOLESTEROL, 69 MG.

Swordfish with Roasted Onion Vinaigrette

This vinaigrette can also be used on cold poached chicken breasts.

VARIATION: Try this recipe with halibut steaks or sea bass fillets instead.
DO-AHEAD: The time-consuming portion of this recipe—roasting the onions for the vinaigrette—can be done a day ahead of time.

4 SERVINGS

3 cups sliced red onions

1 tablespoon olive oil

1 tablespoon fresh thyme leaves or
   1 teaspoon dried

½ cup sliced red bell pepper

1 tablespoon cider vinegar

2 12-ounce pieces swordfish (about 1 inch
   thick), halved
Fresh thyme sprigs

Preheat oven to 400°F. Combine onions, oil and 1 tablespoon thyme in large baking dish. Bake until onions are golden and tender, stirring occasionally, about 40 minutes. *(Can be prepared 1 day ahead. Cover and refrigerate. Reheat in 400°F oven before continuing.)*

Stir bell pepper and vinegar into onions. Season with salt and pepper and push to one side of dish. Sprinkle fish with salt and pepper and arrange alongside vegetables. Bake until fish is opaque, about 10 minutes. Transfer fish to platter. Arrange vegetables over. Garnish with fresh thyme sprigs.

PER SERVING: CALORIES, 221, TOTAL FAT, 9.0, SATURATED FAT, 2.0, CHOLESTEROL, 45 MG.

Hot off the Grill

The great thing about the grill is how it simplifies dinner and flavors foods all at the same time. After just minutes, ribs, chops and more are crisp, brown and delicious. And there's no washing up.

Mustard-glazed Spareribs

Serve with baked beans and coleslaw. Any leftovers are wonderful cold or can be wrapped in foil and reheated in the oven.

VARIATION: This glaze would also work well for grilling up to four chicken breast halves with skin and bones (skip the baking step).

DO-AHEAD: Note that the ribs can be baked and the glaze can be made in advance, leaving only the grilling to do right before dinner.

1½ tablepoons minced fresh rosemary

4 medium garlic cloves, minced

2 racks (about 6 pounds) pork spareribs

⅔ cup (firmly packed) dark brown sugar

½ cup coarse-grained Dijon mustard

⅓ cup cider vinegar

2 tablespoons molasses

1 tablespoon dry mustard

Fresh rosemary sprigs (optional)

4 SERVINGS

Preheat oven to 350°F. Rub minced rosemary and garlic onto both sides of ribs. Sprinkle with **salt** and pepper. Arrange, meaty side down, on baking sheet. Bake 1 hour, turning once.

Combine brown sugar, Dijon, vinegar, molasses and dry mustard in heavy large saucepan. Bring to simmer over low heat, stirring. Cool glaze. *(Can be prepared 1 day ahead. Cool completely. Cover ribs and glaze separately with plastic and refrigerate.)*

Prepare barbecue (medium heat). Place ribs on grill rack, meaty side up. Spread top with ⅓ of glaze. Cook until bottom side is crisp, about 5 minutes. Turn, spread second side with glaze and cook until bottom side is crisp, about 5 minutes. Turn, spread top with glaze and cook until bottom side is glazed, about 5 minutes. Transfer to platter. Cut into individual ribs. Garnish with fresh rosemary sprigs, if desired, and serve immediately.

Grilled Pork Chops
with Bourbon-Mustard Glaze

Corn muffins, coleslaw and green beans would round out this main course.

VARIATION: Turkey scallops would work well here instead of pork chops.

DO-AHEAD: Prepare the glaze ahead of time and dinner can be ready in less than ten minutes.

4 SERVINGS

⅔ cup bottled chili sauce

½ cup bourbon

3 tablespoons Dijon mustard

3 tablespoons reduced-sodium soy sauce

8 thin-cut pork rib chops (each
about ¼ to ⅓ inch thick)

Combine chili sauce, bourbon, mustard and soy sauce in heavy medium saucepan. Simmer over medium heat until sauce is reduced enough to coat spoon, whisking occasionally, about 4 minutes. *(Can be prepared 4 days ahead. Cover and refrigerate.)*

Prepare barbecue (medium-high heat). Sprinkle both sides of chops with salt and pepper. Brush 1 side of chops generously with sauce. Place chops, sauce side down, on grill. Brush chops generously with remaining sauce. Grill until cooked through and glazed, about 3 minutes per side.

Scallop Brochettes
with Mango-Tarragon Salsa

Buttered orzo and grilled pattypan squash are great with the scallops.

VARIATION: Shrimp can stand in for the scallops; the salsa can be made with fresh basil, mint or cilantro instead of tarragon.

DO-AHEAD: The dressing and salsa can be made in the morning.

¼ cup olive oil

2 tablespoons chopped fresh tarragon or
  2 teaspoons dried

3 tablespoons fresh lime juice

2 teaspoons grated lime peel

1⅓ cups diced peeled mango

⅔ cup diced red bell pepper

⅔ cup diced sweet onion (such as Vidalia or Maui)

24 sea scallops

Whisk first 4 ingredients in medium bowl to blend. Transfer 2 tablespoons dressing to small bowl and reserve. Mix mango, bell pepper and onion into remaining dressing in medium bowl; season salsa with salt and pepper. *(Can be made 8 hours ahead. Cover salsa and dressing separately and refrigerate.)*

Prepare barbecue (medium high heat). Thread 6 scallops onto each of 4 skewers. Brush reserved 2 tablespoons dressing over scallops; sprinkle with salt and pepper. Grill scallops until just opaque in center, about 3 minutes per side. Transfer scallops to plates. Spoon salsa alongside and serve.

Rosemary Chicken and
Summer Squash Brochettes

Serve the brochettes atop rice and offer cherry tomatoes with ranch dressing on the side. End the meal with a peach pie from the bakery.

VARIATION: Substitute one 14-ounce pork tenderloin cut into 1½-inch pieces for the chicken, and zucchini for the pattypan squash.

4 SERVINGS

¼ cup extra-virgin olive oil

2 tablespoons fresh lemon juice

2 tablespoons chopped fresh rosemary or
  1 tablespoon dried

4 garlic cloves, minced

2 teaspoons grated lemon peel

4 skinless boneless chicken breast halves,
  each cut into 6 pieces

6 large pattypan squash, each quartered

Prepare barbecue (medium-high heat). Whisk first 5 ingredients in medium bowl. Add chicken and squash; toss. Let stand 10 minutes, tossing occasionally.

Alternate 3 chicken pieces with 3 squash pieces on each of 8 skewers. Sprinkle with salt and pepper. Grill until chicken is cooked through and squash is just tender, turning often, 10 minutes.

Grilled Shrimp with Ponzu Sauce

The marinade and sauce for this shrimp takes its name from *ponzu*—a Japanese dipping sauce made with similar ingredients. Garnish purchased sesame noodle salad with chopped green onions and peanuts to serve with this.

VARIATION: Substitute four six-ounce ahi tuna fillets (each one inch thick) for the shrimp.

---

6 tablespoons soy sauce

6 tablespoons mirin (sweet Japanese rice wine), or 6 tablespoons dry Sherry mixed with 2 tablespoons sugar

6 tablespoons fresh lemon juice

¼ cup olive oil

2 tablespoons chopped peeled fresh ginger

2 teaspoons grated lemon peel

20 uncooked extra-large shrimp (about 20 ounces), peeled, deveined

4 cups thinly sliced bok choy or Napa cabbage

4 SERVINGS

Prepare barbecue (medium-high heat). Whisk soy sauce, mirin, lemon juice, oil, ginger and lemon peel in shallow bowl to blend. Add shrimp and stir to coat; marinate 10 minutes.

Drain shrimp marinade into small saucepan and boil 1 minute. Grill shrimp until just opaque in center, turning occasionally, about 3 minutes.

Divide bok choy among plates and drizzle with some of warm marinade. Top with shrimp. Serve, passing remaining marinade as sauce, if desired.

Grilled Halibut with Warm Tomato Compote

Quarter four small zucchini lengthwise and grill to serve with the halibut. Round out the menu with steamed baby potatoes seasoned with pepper.

VARIATION: Use swordfish or sea bass instead of halibut.

DO-AHEAD: Note that the tomato compote can be prepared ahead of time.

3 tablespoons butter

4 6- to 7-ounce halibut fillets (each about 1 inch thick)

¼ cup chopped shallots

2 cups chopped plum tomatoes (about 10 ounces)

⅓ cup dry white wine

2 tablespoons (packed) chopped fresh tarragon or 2 teaspoons dried

Melt butter in heavy large skillet. Brush fish on both sides with half of butter. Sprinkle fish with salt and pepper. Add shallots to butter remaining in skillet. Cook over high heat 1 minute. Add tomatoes to skillet and cook until juices evaporate, stirring occasionally, about 2 minutes. Add wine and tarragon and boil until compote is thick, about 1 minute. Remove from heat; season with salt and pepper. *(Can be prepared 2 hours ahead. Cover with foil to keep warm.)*

Prepare barbecue (medium-high heat). Grill fish until just opaque in center, about 4 minutes per side. Transfer to plates. Spoon compote alongside fish and serve immediately.

East-West Barbecued Chicken

Offer baked potatoes and grilled corn on the cob with dinner.

VARIATION: Use lamb rib chops or ¾-inch-thick pork rib chops, if you like.

4 SERVINGS

---

2 2½- to 3-pound chickens, each cut into
    4 pieces, wings removed

4 teaspoons Dijon mustard

½ cup orange juice

2 tablespoons olive oil

½ teaspoon dried crushed red pepper

½ cup bottled chili sauce

½ cup hoisin sauce

Place chicken in large baking pan. Sprinkle with salt and pepper. Place mustard in small bowl. Whisk in orange juice, oil and dried red pepper. Pour over chicken, turning chicken to coat. Let stand 20 minutes. Combine chili sauce and hoisin sauce in small bowl.

Prepare barbecue (medium-high heat). Grill chicken until just cooked through, about 10 minutes per side. Brush one side with chili-hoisin mixture and grill until beginning to brown, about 3 minutes. Brush second side with chili-hoisin mixture and grill until beginning to brown. Serve chicken immediately.

GRILLING ADD-ONS

Cooking on the grill adds a lot of flavor—fast—without much effort. To add even more, use marinades and rubs, dipping sauces, herb butters and salsas. Keep it simple and tasty.

FOR GRILLED FISH

- Herb Butter: softened butter mixed with dill, chives or parsley.
- Cucumber Salsa: chopped cucumbers, chopped fresh chives or dill, white wine vinegar, salt and pepper.
- Tomato-Green Onion Salsa: chopped seeded tomatoes, chopped green onions, chopped parsley, balsamic vinegar, salt and pepper.
- Spicy Dipping Sauce: orange juice, cider vinegar, ground cumin, chopped cilantro, salt and pepper.

FOR GRILLED CHICKEN

- Asian Dipping Sauce: soy sauce, minced fresh ginger, sesame oil.
- Mediterranean Dipping Sauce: olive oil, red wine vinegar, chopped fresh thyme or oregano, minced garlic.
- Tomatillo Salsa: diced tomatillos (peeled and cooked in boiling water one minute), chopped white onion and chopped cilantro.

FOR GRILLED MEATS

- Rosemary Dipping Sauce: olive oil, red wine vinegar, chopped fresh rosemary, coarsely ground pepper.
- Italian Drizzle: olive oil, balsamic vinegar, coarse black pepper.
- Mushroom Topping: sautéed chopped wild mushrooms (portobello, chanterelle or shiitake), black pepper.

Grilled T-Bone Steaks Florentine

A marinade of olive oil, parsley, balsamic vinegar, fresh rosemary and garlic flavors steaks in the classic Italian tradition. Serve buttered pasta and steamed broccoli alongside. End with grilled bananas brushed with honey.

VARIATION: Lamb leg steaks would work well here too.
DO-AHEAD: The steak can marinate for up to eight hours.

2 SERVINGS

⅓ cup olive oil

2 tablespoons minced fresh parsley

1½ tablespoons balsamic vinegar

1 teaspoon minced fresh rosemary

1 garlic clove, minced

2 ¾- to 1-inch-thick T-bone steaks

Whisk first 5 ingredients in shallow pan to blend. Add steaks, turning to coat both sides. Cover and refrigerate at least 1 hour and up to 8 hours.

Prepare barbecue (medium-high heat). Remove steaks from marinade and sprinkle with salt and pepper. Grill to desired doneness, about 4 minutes per side for medium-rare.

Grilled Tuna with Salade Niçoise

The traditional *salade niçoise* contains tomatoes, black olives, garlic, anchovies, green beans, onions, tuna, hard-boiled eggs and herbs; this new twist also has potatoes, and instead of the tuna being in the salad, the salad is served alongside grilled tuna.

VARIATION: Salmon or sea bass fillets (½ inch thick) could replace the tuna.
DO-AHEAD: The salad can be prepared ahead of time.

---

4 ⅓- to ½-pound tuna steaks
 Olive oil
 Fresh lemon juice

8 small White Rose potatoes, halved lengthwise
1 pound green beans, trimmed, cut into thirds

3 tablespoons white wine vinegar
3 tablespoons Dijon mustard
4 small shallots, minced
¾ cup olive oil
4 teaspoons minced fresh thyme or
 1 teaspoon dried
⅔ cup Niçois olives*

2 tomatoes, sliced

4 SERVINGS

Rub tuna steaks with oil and lemon juice. Let stand while preparing salad.

Add potatoes and beans to large pot of boiling salted water. Cook beans until just crisp-tender. Remove with slotted spoon. Rinse under cold water; drain well. Continue cooking potatoes until tender. Drain. Cut crosswise into ½-inch-thick slices. Transfer potato slices to medium bowl.

Combine vinegar, mustard and shallots in another medium bowl. Gradually whisk in ¾ cup olive oil. Mix in thyme. Season to taste with salt and pepper. Toss ⅓ of dressing with potatoes. Cool. Add beans, olives and half of remaining dressing to potatoes and toss to combine. *(Can be made 4 hours ahead. Cover and chill salad and fish separately. Keep dressing covered at room temperature.)*

Prepare barbecue (medium-high heat). Sprinkle tuna steaks with salt and pepper. Grill until just cooked through, about 4 minutes per side. Divide fish and salad among plates. Garnish with tomatoes. Serve, passing remaining dressing separately.

*Small brine-cured black olives, available at Italian markets, specialty foods stores and some supermarkets.

Make-ahead Casseroles

You know it's going to be a busy night, with little time to cook. The solution is to make dinner ahead, then heat and serve. Casseroles are just the thing.

Baked Penne with Sausage, Zucchini and Fontina

Kids love this cheesy pasta bake—even with the chunks of zucchini. It's a sneaky way to get them to eat their vegetables.

VARIATION: Replace the sausage and Fontina with diced ham and Jarlsberg cheese.
DO-AHEAD: The casserole can be prepared a day ahead and baked just before serving.

---

3 medium zucchini, trimmed, halved lengthwise

1 tablespoon olive oil

½ pound Italian hot sausage, casings removed

1 onion, chopped

1 cup whipping cream

1 teaspoon dried oregano

½ pound Fontina cheese, grated

½ pound penne or other tubular pasta

Fresh oregano sprigs (optional)

Preheat oven to 375°F. Lightly oil 2½- to 3-quart deep casserole dish. Cut each zucchini half in thirds lengthwise, then crosswise into 1½-inch-long pieces.

Heat oil in heavy large skillet over medium heat. Add sausage and cook until no longer pink, breaking up with fork. Using slotted spoon, transfer to bowl. Add onion to skillet and cook until beginning to soften, stirring occasionally, about 5 minutes. Add zucchini. Sauté until almost tender, about 8 minutes. Return sausage to skillet. Add whipping cream and oregano and bring sauce to boil. Add half of Fontina cheese to sauce and stir just until melted.

Meanwhile, cook pasta in large pot of boiling salted water until tender but still firm to bite. Drain well. Return to pot. Add sauce and stir to coat. Season to taste with salt and pepper. Transfer to prepared casserole dish. Top with remaining cheese. *(Can be prepared 1 day ahead. Cover and refrigerate. Bring to room temperature before continuing.)* Bake until heated through, about 15 minutes. Garnish with fresh oregano sprigs, if desired, and serve hot.

Polenta, Beef and Bean Pie

Ready-made polenta, bottled salsa and canned beans make this recipe a snap to prepare.

VARIATION: Ground lamb or turkey can be used in place of the ground beef.
DO-AHEAD: The casserole can be prepared ahead; bake just before serving.

8 SERVINGS

1 pound ground beef

1½ tablespoons chili powder

1 tablespoon ground cumin

1 16-ounce bottle spicy salsa

1 15- to 16-ounce can refried beans

1 14½-ounce can low-salt chicken broth

½ cup chopped fresh cilantro

2 1-pound rolls prepared polenta, sliced into
⅓-inch-thick rounds

3 cups shredded sharp cheddar cheese

Sauté beef in heavy large pot over medium-high heat until no longer pink, breaking up with back of fork, about 3 minutes. Add chili powder and cumin; stir 1 minute. Add salsa, beans and broth. Simmer until mixture thickens, about 10 minutes. Mix in ¼ cup cilantro; season with salt and pepper.

Oil 13x9x2-inch glass baking dish. Place half of polenta in dish. Top with sauce and 1½ cups cheese, then remaining polenta, cheese and cilantro. *(Can be made 2 days ahead. Cover with foil; chill.)*

Preheat oven to 350°F. Bake freshly assembled pie, uncovered, until heated through and sauce bubbles, about 35 minutes; or bake refrigerated pie, covered, 20 minutes, then uncover and bake until heated through, about 35 minutes longer. Serve hot.

Contemporary Tuna-Noodle Casserole

Reduced-fat cream cheese, low-fat milk and water-packed canned tuna are the secrets to this updated, lighter take on a 1950s favorite.

VARIATION: Fusilli pasta or large shells would work in place of farfalle.
DO-AHEAD: The tuna mixture can be made a full day before, and the entire casserole can be put together hours ahead of time. Top with chips and bake just before serving.

---

6 SERVINGS

Nonstick vegetable oil spray
¼ cup dry white wine
4 teaspoons cornstarch
⅓ cup all purpose flour
1½ cups low-fat milk
1 cup canned low-salt chicken broth
2 teaspoons minced fresh thyme or
  1 teaspoon dried
2 tablespoons reduced-fat cream cheese

1 6-ounce can solid white tuna packed in
  water, undrained
1 6-ounce can chunk light tuna packed in
  water, undrained
1 cup frozen petite peas, unthawed

8 ounces farfalle (bow-tie) pasta

½ cup crushed potato chips (about 1 ounce)

Spray 8x8x2-inch glass baking dish with nonstick spray. Whisk wine and cornstarch in small bowl to blend. Whisk flour in heavy medium saucepan to remove any lumps. Gradually add milk to flour, whisking until smooth. Add broth and thyme and whisk over medium heat until liquid thickens and boils, about 4 minutes. Add cornstarch mixture and whisk until liquid boils and is smooth, about 1 minute. Remove from heat. Add cream cheese and whisk until melted. Stir in both cans of tuna with their liquid and frozen peas. Season to taste with salt and pepper. *(Can be prepared 1 day ahead. Cover and refrigerate.)*

Meanwhile, cook pasta in large pot of boiling salted water until tender but still firm to bite, stirring occasionally. Drain pasta. Return to pot. *(Can be prepared 6 hours ahead; chill.)*

Preheat oven to 400°F. Add tuna mixture to pasta; stir to blend well. Transfer to prepared baking dish. Sprinkle with potato chips. Bake casserole until top is golden and sauce bubbles around edges of dish, about 25 minutes. Serve hot.

Hearty Moussaka with Low-fat White Sauce

This lighter take on the classic is topped with a low-fat white sauce instead of the rich béchamel sauce usually used. Loaded with fresh vegetables and topped with Parmesan cheese, it will satisfy the biggest hunger.

VARIATION: Use ground lamb in place of ground beef.
DO-AHEAD: Start making this casserole a day ahead, if you wish.

Nonstick olive oil spray

2 12-ounce eggplants, peeled, each cut lengthwise in half, then cut crosswise into ½-inch-thick slices

1½ pounds medium zucchini, trimmed, cut into ¼-inch-thick rounds

1 pound red-skinned new potatoes, cut into ¼-inch-thick rounds

1 tablespoon olive oil

2 cups chopped onions

3 garlic cloves, minced

2 teaspoons dried oregano

1 pound lean ground beef sirloin or ground round

1 28-ounce can whole tomatoes in juice

3 tablespoons tomato paste

½ cup plain dry white breadcrumbs

2 large egg whites, beaten to blend

¼ teaspoon ground cinnamon

Low-fat White Sauce (see recipe)

2 tablespoons grated Parmesan cheese

Preheat oven to 425°F. Spray 2 large baking sheets with nonstick spray. Arrange eggplant slices and half of zucchini rounds, overlapping slightly, on 1 baking sheet. Arrange potato rounds and remaining zucchini, overlapping slightly, on second baking sheet. Spray vegetables generously with nonstick spray. Sprinkle with salt and pepper. Bake until tender and beginning to brown, about 40 minutes. Remove from oven and cool. *(Can be prepared 1 day ahead. Cover and refrigerate.)*

Heat oil in large nonstick skillet over medium heat. Add onions and garlic; sauté until onions are tender, about 7 minutes. Stir in oregano. Add beef; sauté until brown, breaking up with back of spoon. Add tomatoes with juices and tomato paste, breaking up tomatoes with back of spoon. Simmer until mixture thickens slightly, about 15 minutes. Season to taste with salt and pepper. Remove from heat. *(Can be prepared 1 day ahead. Cool, cover and chill. Rewarm over low heat before continuing.)* Mix in ¼ cup breadcrumbs, egg whites and cinnamon.

Preheat oven to 375°F. Spray 13x9x2-inch glass baking dish with nonstick spray. Sprinkle remaining ¼ cup breadcrumbs over bottom of dish. Arrange potatoes in prepared dish. Spoon half of beef mixture over. Arrange eggplant slices over. Spoon remaining beef mixture over. Top with all of zucchini, overlapping slightly.

Pour warm Low-fat White Sauce over moussaka. Sprinkle cheese over. Bake until top is golden brown, about 55 minutes. Let stand 15 minutes. Cut into squares and serve.

Low fat White Sauce

  6 tablespoons all purpose flour
  3 cups low-fat (1%) milk
  ¼ teaspoon ground nutmeg
  ⅓ cup grated Parmesan cheese
  1 large egg, beaten to blend
  1 teaspoon butter

Whisk flour in heavy medium saucepan to remove any lumps. Gradually add 1 cup milk, whisking until smooth. Add remaining 2 cups milk and nutmeg; whisk over medium heat until mixture thickens and boils, about 10 minutes. Remove from heat. Whisk in Parmesan, egg and butter. Season with salt and pepper.

CASSEROLE HOW-TOS

Easy to make and serve, casseroles rose to the top of the charts in the 1950s, beloved because they got the cook in and out of the kitchen fast. Those versions were largely made from a variety of canned goods; today's casseroles are fresh, tasty and as convenient as ever. Some tips to keep in mind.

- Baking Dish: Most casserole dishes are made of ovenproof glass, porcelain or earthenware. You also find enameled cast iron and aluminum versions. Glass, though it's not an ideal heat conductor, is one of your best options, as it retains heat well (so the casserole stays hot longer) and does not interact with certain foods (tomatoes, eggs and wine, in particular), as aluminum does. Glass can also go right into the microwave for thawing or reheating (do not use glass, porcelain or earthenware on top of the stove). Enameled cast iron is an excellent heat conductor, but it can chip, and you can't use it in the microwave.

- Freezing: Cool the casserole after baking. Cover with plastic wrap, then heavy-duty aluminum foil. Label the dish with the following information: type of food, number of servings, date prepared, and cooking or reheating instructions.

- Thawing: Most casseroles are best when thawed in the refrigerator overnight, then reheated in the oven. In a pinch, you can thaw a casserole in the microwave, then reheat it. Be sure to turn the dish often, because the microwave tends to thaw the edges of the casserole first, leaving the center frozen.

Corn and Green Chili Tamale Casserole

This spicy casserole can also be made in a microwave: Cook it on high until heated through and juices bubble, about 15 minutes; rotate the dish several times, if necessary.

VARIATION: Use green chili and cheese tamales for a vegetarian version of this casserole.
DO-AHEAD: Make the casserole a day ahead, then bake it just before serving.

4 SERVINGS

6 4-ounce frozen chicken or beef tamales	1½ teaspoons chili powder
1 10-ounce package frozen white or yellow corn, unthawed	1 teaspoon ground cumin
1 4-ounce can diced mild green chilies	¼ teaspoon salt
3 green onions, chopped	¼ teaspoon ground black pepper
1 cup chopped fresh cilantro	2 cups grated Monterey Jack cheese
1 cup whipping cream	
1 7-ounce can salsa verde	Avocado wedges
	Additional salsa verde (optional)

Place frozen tamales in microwave and cook on high until thawed, about 5 minutes. Remove husks. Cut tamales in half lengthwise. Place in single layer in 10-inch-diameter glass pie dish. Sprinkle with frozen corn, chilies, green onions and ½ cup cilantro. Whisk cream, salsa verde, chili powder, cumin, salt and pepper in medium bowl to blend. Drizzle over casserole. Sprinkle grated cheese over top. *(Can be prepared 1 day ahead. Cover and refrigerate.)*

Preheat oven to 375°F. Bake casserole until heated through and bubbling, about 35 minutes. Sprinkle with ½ cup cilantro. Serve with avocado and additional salsa, if desired.

Super-Fast Spinach, Pesto and Cheese Lasagna

In this contemporary and meatless take on lasagna, "no-boil" or "oven-ready" noodles eliminate a step, and bottled pasta sauce stands in for homemade.

DO-AHEAD: Put the lasagna together the night or morning before you plan to serve it; while the lasagna bakes, toss a salad to go with it.

---

3 cups ricotta cheese

1 cup shredded Parmesan cheese

1 large egg

2 10-ounce packages frozen chopped spinach, thawed, squeezed dry

1 7-ounce package prepared pesto

4 cups bottled chunky pasta sauce

12 no-boil lasagna noodles from one 8-ounce package

2 cups grated Fontina or mozzarella cheese

8 SERVINGS

Blend ricotta and Parmesan in medium bowl. Season cheeses with salt and pepper; stir in egg. Blend spinach and pesto in another medium bowl.

Brush 13x9x2-inch glass baking dish with oil. Spread 1 cup pasta sauce in prepared dish. Arrange 3 noodles side by side atop sauce. Spread 1¼ cups cheese mixture over in thin layer. Drop ⅓ of spinach mixture over by spoonfuls. Repeat layering with sauce, noodles, cheese mixture and spinach mixture 2 more times. Top with remaining 3 noodles and 1 cup sauce. Cover lasagna with foil. (Can be prepared 1 day ahead; refrigerate.)

Preheat oven to 350°F. Bake lasagna, covered, 35 minutes. Uncover; sprinkle with Fontina cheese. Bake until lasagna is heated through, sauce bubbles and cheese on top is melted, about 15 minutes longer. Let stand 10 minutes before serving.

Zucchini Parmigiana with Tomato Sauce

Serve this old-fashioned, appealing entrée with spaghetti tossed with olive oil.

DO-AHEAD: The entire casserole can be prepared a day ahead; bake just before serving.

1½ teaspoons olive oil

1 medium onion, chopped

1 to 2 tablespoons water

1 garlic clove, minced

2 teaspoons dried basil, crumbled

1 teaspoon dried oregano, crumbled

1 teaspoon fennel seeds

½ pound extra-lean ground beef

½ cup dry white wine

1 28-ounce can whole peeled tomatoes, drained (juices reserved), chopped

1 tablespoon tomato paste

6 large zucchini, each cut lengthwise into 5 slices

8 tablespoons freshly grated Parmesan cheese

Heat oil in heavy medium saucepan over medium heat. Add onion and sauté until tender, adding 1 to 2 tablespoons water if onion sticks, about 3 minutes. Add garlic, basil, oregano and fennel seeds and sauté 1 minute. Add beef and cook until brown, breaking up with fork, about 4 minutes. Add wine and bring to boil. Add tomatoes with juices and tomato paste. Simmer until sauce is reduced to 3 cups, stirring occasionally, about 1½ hours. Season sauce to taste with salt and pepper. *(Can be made 2 days ahead. Cover and refrigerate.)*

Cook zucchini in large pot of boiling salted water until tender, about 2 minutes. Drain. Rinse under cold water. Transfer zucchini to paper towels and drain well.

Spread 1 cup sauce in 9x13-inch glass baking dish. Top with 15 zucchini slices, overlapping slightly. Sprinkle with 2 tablespoons cheese. Season with salt and pepper. Repeat layering, using 1 cup sauce, remaining 15 zucchini slices and 2 tablespoons cheese. Spread remaining 1 cup sauce over. Sprinkle with remaining cheese. *(Can be prepared 1 day ahead. Cover and chill.)*

Preheat oven to 350°F. Bake zucchini until top bubbles and is golden brown, about 30 minutes.

Potato and Salmon Casserole

Canned salmon and potatoes are good sources of calcium. Serve with an endive salad.

DO-AHEAD: Make this casserole up to four hours ahead of time.

6 SERVINGS

Nonstick vegetable oil spray

1 14.75-ounce can pink salmon, drained

2½ pounds russet potatoes, peeled, cut into
    1-inch pieces

1 cup milk

4 ounces soft fresh goat cheese
   (such as Montrachet)

3 tablespoons (packed) freshly grated
   Parmesan cheese

2 large eggs

½ cup chopped green onions

Preheat oven to 400°F. Spray 10-inch-diameter glass pie dish with nonstick spray. Separate salmon into chunks, leaving bones intact (bones are very soft and will blend). Remove black pieces of skin; discard.

Cook potatoes in large pot of boiling salted water until very tender, about 20 minutes. Drain. Transfer potatoes to large bowl. Add milk, goat cheese and 2 tablespoons Parmesan cheese. Using electric mixer, beat until almost smooth. Season with salt and pepper. Beat in eggs. Stir in salmon and green onions. Transfer mixture to prepared dish. Sprinkle with remaining 1 tablespoon Parmesan cheese. Bake casserole until golden and heated through, about 45 minutes. *(Can be prepared 4 hours ahead. Cover with plastic and refrigerate.)* Serve warm.

Fallback Favorites

Everybody has their favorite fallback recipes, those dishes you make from memory, the ones that taste great every time. Here are nine candidates for that special designation, recipes that are as simple as they are delicious, as easy as they are appealing.

Broiled Salmon with
Avocado and Lime Relish

It takes just 20 minutes to make this impressive-looking and great-tasting main course. Couscous is a quick accompaniment.

VARIATION: One 12- to 14-ounce salmon fillet would work just as well. You could also substitute sea bass or red snapper, if desired.

2 SERVINGS

2 6- to 7-ounce salmon fillets	1 firm but ripe avocado, diced
1 tablespoon plus ¼ cup olive oil	1 bunch fresh chives, chopped
½ lime	1 tablespoon fresh lime juice

Rub salmon with 1 tablespoon oil. Squeeze lime over. Let stand while preparing relish.

Combine avocado, ¼ cup oil, chives and 1 tablespoon lime juice. Season with salt and pepper.

Preheat broiler. Place salmon, skin side down, on foil-lined baking sheet. Sprinkle with salt and pepper. Broil without turning until just opaque, approximately 10 to 15 minutes. Transfer salmon to plates. Spoon avocado relish over and serve immediately.

Cornish Game Hens
with Maple-Mustard Glaze

Wild rice and winter squash are perfect with this easy and elegant entrée. There is very little preparation for this recipe, but the hens need to roast for one hour.

VARIATION: Use two large chicken breasts with ribs or legs with thighs instead.

2 TO 4 SERVINGS

2 tablespoons pure maple syrup

1½ tablespoons butter

1 tablespoon Dijon mustard

1 teaspoon dried thyme

2 Cornish game hens

Preheat oven to 350°F. Combine first 4 ingredients in small saucepan. Cook over low heat until butter melts, stirring until well combined. Remove from heat.

Pat hens dry. Tie legs together to hold shape. Place in small baking pan. Sprinkle with salt and pepper. Brush with maple mixture. Roast until juices run clear when hens are pierced in thickest part of thigh, basting occasionally with glaze, about 1 hour. Serve immediately.

Salt- and Pepper-crusted Pork

Offer cranberry sauce, mashed potatoes and steamed broccoli with this entrée.

VARIATION: This rub would also be great on thick pork chops.
DO-AHEAD: Note that the pork can marinate overnight.

4 teaspoons pepper

2 teaspoons salt

2 teaspoons dried rosemary

2 large garlic cloves, minced

2 12-ounce (about) pork tenderloins

2 tablespoons olive oil

Combine pepper, salt, rosemary and garlic in small bowl. Rub over both tenderloins. Let pork stand at least 15 minutes. *(Can be prepared 1 day ahead. Cover and chill.)*

Preheat oven to 400°F. Heat oil in heavy large ovenproof skillet over high heat. Add tenderloins and brown on all sides, about 6 minutes. Transfer skillet with pork to oven and roast until pork is cooked through, turning occasionally, about 20 minutes. Slice and serve.

A FEW OF OUR FAVORITE THINGS

Everybody has a repertoire of dishes they can make by heart, specialties that are guaranteed to taste good every time. They don't require a grocery list and they don't require a recipe. They're the dishes you turn to time and again   the chef's specials in your kitchen. Here are some of the favorites at *Bon Appétit*.

- Chicken brushed with butter, rolled in breadcrumbs, seasoned with Parmesan cheese and pepper and baked.
- Roast chicken with roasted herbed potatoes.
- Broiled lamb chops with fresh mint and garlic.
- Pan-fried steak with balsamic glaze (deglaze the pan with balsamic vinegar, stir in a pat of butter).
- Baked salmon with herb butter.
- Macaroni and cheese (as easy as cheese sauce and cooked macaroni, mixed and baked).
- Pot roast with carrots, onions and potatoes.
- Meat loaf.
- Grilled sausages with cooked red cabbage.

Turkey Hash
with Sweet Potatoes and Turnips

Purchase a roasted turkey leg to use in this recipe—or use leftover turkey.

VARIATION: Use chicken and russet potatoes in place of turkey and sweet potatoes.

3 cups canned low-salt chicken broth

1 bay leaf

1 8-ounce red-skinned sweet potato (yam), peeled and quartered lengthwise

½ pound turnips, peeled and quartered

2 tablespoons (¼ stick) butter

2 large onions, chopped

4 ounces mushrooms, quartered

2 cups ½-inch pieces skinned roasted turkey or chicken

¼ cup whipping cream

1 large egg yolk

1 teaspoon minced fresh tarragon or ½ teaspoon dried

Additional minced fresh tarragon or dried

Combine chicken broth and bay leaf in large saucepan. Bring to boil. Add sweet potato and turnips. Reduce heat, cover and simmer until vegetables are almost tender, about 12 minutes. Using slotted spoon, remove vegetables. Simmer broth until reduced to 1½ cups, about 15 minutes. Discard bay leaf. Cut vegetables into ½-inch pieces; set aside.

Melt butter in heavy large skillet over medium-low heat. Add onions and sauté until golden brown, about 10 minutes. Increase heat to high and add mushrooms, turnips and sweet potato. Sauté until vegetables are golden brown, about 4 minutes. Add chicken broth and boil until reduced by half, about 5 minutes. Mix in turkey and stir to heat through. Remove from heat. Whisk cream and egg yolk in small bowl to blend. Add to turkey mixture. Mix in 1 teaspoon tarragon. Place over low heat and stir until sauce thickens, about 30 seconds (do not boil). Season to taste with salt and pepper. Sprinkle with additional minced tarragon and serve immediately.

Cajun Meat Loaf

Sautéed greens (such as collard or mustard) would go well with this southern take on meat loaf. Leftovers make a great sandwich.

DO-AHEAD: Put the meat loaf together ahead of time and bake just before serving.

2 tablespoons (¼ stick) butter

½ large onion, chopped

½ cup chopped green bell pepper

1 teaspoon salt

¾ teaspoon cayenne pepper

½ teaspoon dried thyme

½ teaspoon pepper

¼ teaspoon ground cumin

1 pound lean ground beef

1 large egg, beaten to blend

½ cup dry breadcrumbs

½ cup ketchup

1 teaspoon Worcestershire sauce

Melt butter in heavy medium skillet over medium-low heat. Add next 7 ingredients and cook until vegetables are tender, stirring frequently, about 10 minutes.

Combine meat, egg, breadcrumbs, ¼ cup ketchup and Worcestershire sauce in medium bowl. Stir in sautéed vegetables. Form mixture into loaf 1¾ inches high and 5 inches wide in baking dish. *(Can be prepared 2 hours ahead. Cover and refrigerate.)* Preheat oven to 375°F. Bake 20 minutes. Spread top with remaining ¼ cup ketchup and bake 40 minutes longer.

Bacon, Green Onion and Cheese Tart

This quiche-like savory tart is easy and sophisticated. Pair it with mixed baby greens tossed with a simple red wine vinaigrette.

VARIATION: Other meat and cheese combinations that would work well in this tart include pancetta and Fontina cheese or diced kielbasa with Gruyère; a meatless version could be made with sautéed mushrooms and Brie cheese (remove the rind).

DO-AHEAD: Note that the tart can be served hot or at room temperature, so it can be made ahead and cooled before serving, if desired.

4 SERVINGS

1 frozen 9-inch deep-dish pie crust

6 slices bacon, cut into ⅓-inch-wide pieces

1 tablespoon (about) butter

1 bunch green onions, sliced

3 large eggs

1½ cups half and half

½ teaspoon salt

Ground nutmeg

½ pound Port-Salut or Muenster cheese, trimmed, grated

Preheat oven to 400°F. Thaw pie crust 10 minutes. Bake crust until pale golden, about 12 minutes. Transfer to rack and cool. Reduce oven temperature to 375°F.

Cook bacon in heavy medium skillet over medium-low heat until crisp. Using slotted spoon, transfer bacon to paper towels to drain. Sprinkle bacon over crust. Add enough butter to skillet to measure 1 tablespoon fat. Add green onions and sprinkle with pepper. Sauté over medium heat until tender, about 2 minutes. Transfer to medium bowl. Add eggs, half and half, salt and nutmeg to bowl; whisk to blend. Sprinkle cheese over crust. Pour in egg mixture. Sprinkle tart liberally with pepper. Place tart on baking sheet. Cook until beginning to puff and knife inserted into center comes out clean, about 40 minutes (cover edges with foil if browning too quickly). Serve tart hot or at room temperature.

Lemon and Tarragon Baked Chicken

What to do with chicken breasts? Try this quick breadcrumb coating. Serve with steamed asparagus and white or wild rice.

DO-AHEAD: Prepare the chicken up to four hours in advance, then bake for an hour. Use that time to put together any side dishes.

½ cup (1 stick) unsalted butter	1 tablespoon grated lemon peel	6 SERVINGS
2 large garlic cloves, minced	1 teaspoon dried tarragon	
2 tablespoons Dijon mustard	6 large chicken breast halves	
1 cup dry breadcrumbs		

Line large baking pan with foil. Melt butter in heavy medium skillet over low heat. Add garlic and sauté 1 minute. Remove from heat and stir in mustard. Mix breadcrumbs, lemon peel and tarragon on plate. Place chicken in butter mixture; turn to coat. Place chicken in crumbs; turn to coat completely. Arrange chicken, skin side up, in prepared pan. Sprinkle with salt and pepper. *(Can be prepared 4 hours ahead. Cover and refrigerate.)* Preheat oven to 375°F. Bake chicken until cooked through, basting occasionally with pan drippings, about 1 hour. Serve hot or at room temperature.

Steaks with Brandy, Shallot and Mustard Sauce

Serve with fries and sautéed green beans. Add ice cream for dessert.

VARIATION: Almost any kind of steak will work in place of the filet mignons; you'll need to adjust the cooking time according to thickness and personal preference.

2 SERVINGS

3 tablespoons butter

1 tablespoon vegetable oil

2 1- to 1¼-inch-thick beef filet mignons

2 large shallots, sliced

3 tablespoons brandy

1 cup canned beef broth

1 teaspoon Dijon mustard

Chopped fresh chives

Melt 1 tablespoon butter with oil in heavy large skillet over medium-high heat. Sprinkle steaks with salt and pepper. Add to skillet and sear 2 minutes per side. Reduce heat to medium and cook to desired doneness, about 1 minute longer per side for medium-rare. Transfer steaks to platter. Cover.

Wipe out skillet. Add 1 tablespoon butter and melt over medium heat. Add shallots and sauté 1 minute. Remove from heat; cool 1 minute. Add brandy. Ignite with match. When flames subside, add broth. Boil over high heat until syrupy, about 8 minutes. Whisk in mustard and remaining 1 tablespoon butter. Season to taste with salt and pepper. Spoon sauce over steaks. Garnish with chives.

Sausage and Bell Pepper Bake

Have polenta or pasta on the side; this can also be used to make sub sandwiches.

VARIATION: Use any combination of red, green, yellow or orange bell peppers for this dish; buy what looks best at the market.

---

2   red bell peppers, thinly sliced

2   green bell peppers, thinly sliced

2   medium onions, thinly sliced

4   large garlic cloves, chopped

2   teaspoons dried oregano

¼   teaspoon dried crushed red pepper

2   tablespoons olive oil

2   pounds Italian sweet sausages

Preheat oven to 350°F. Combine first 6 ingredients in 13x9x2-inch glass baking dish. Pour oil over and stir to coat. Season to taste with salt and pepper. Brown sausages in heavy large nonstick skillet over high heat, turning often, about 8 minutes. Arrange on pepper mixture. Bake until sausages are cooked through and peppers are tender, stirring occasionally, about 45 minutes.

Kid Fare, Plus

Cooking for kids comes with its own set of challenges: how to make something your children will like and eat and that you will find interesting and tasty. Begin with this kid-friendly fare.

Lamb Kebabs with Peanut Sauce

Broiling rather than grilling makes the kebabs a year-round favorite. For the finicky, you may want to use less cumin, curry powder and lime juice in the peanut sauce.

VARIATION: Pork or beef would work in place of the lamb.
DO-AHEAD: Prepare the peanut sauce and thread the ingredients onto skewers ahead of time, leaving only the cooking to do before dinner.

¾ cup canned low-salt chicken broth

½ cup milk

1 cup creamy peanut butter (do not use old-fashioned style or freshly ground)

2 teaspoons ground cumin

2 teaspoons curry powder

1 to 2 tablespoons fresh lime juice

14 ounces boneless leg of lamb, cut into twelve 1½-inch cubes

1 medium red onion, cut into 12 pieces

1 small red bell pepper, cut into 12 squares

4 12-inch-long wooden skewers, soaked in water 30 minutes

Freshly steamed rice

Bring broth and milk to simmer in heavy small saucepan over medium heat. Add peanut butter and stir until smooth and heated through. Mix in cumin, curry powder and lime juice to taste. Season with salt and pepper. Remove from heat. *(Can be prepared 2 days ahead. Cover and refrigerate. Rewarm sauce over low heat, stirring until heated through.)*

Preheat broiler. Alternate 3 lamb cubes, 3 onion pieces and 3 bell pepper squares on each skewer. Sprinkle with salt and pepper. Brush kebabs with some of peanut sauce. Broil to desired doneness, about 5 minutes per side for medium-rare. Serve kebabs immediately with steamed rice, passing remaining peanut sauce separately.

Chicken and Cheese Quesadillas

Purchased guacamole and salsa are good accompaniments. Serve with sliced oranges.

VARIATION: Add sliced smoked (fully cooked) sausages or smoked turkey to these quesadillas.

4 SERVINGS

8 9-inch-diameter (burrito-size) flour tortillas
  Vegetable oil
3 cups (packed) shredded Mexican-blend cheeses

3 cups (packed) shredded Mexican-seasoned
  or other purchased roast chicken
½ cup chopped fresh cilantro

Preheat oven to 375°F. Brush 4 tortillas with oil. Place tortillas, oil side down, on 2 baking sheets. Sprinkle each with ½ cup cheese, ¼ of chicken, ¼ of cilantro, and ¼ cup cheese, leaving ¾-inch border. Top each with 1 tortilla, pressing to adhere; brush top with oil.

Bake quesadillas until filling is heated through and edges begin to crisp, about 10 minutes. Using large metal spatula, turn each over and bake until bottom is crisp, about 5 minutes.

Transfer quesadillas to plates. Cut into wedges and serve.

Not Just Buttered Noodles

When your kids are ready to experiment, start with some of the add-ins here.

VARIATION: This is a great recipe to embellish. Add ham cubes, diced cooked chicken, sausage, frozen peas or any other ingredients your children like.

4 SERVINGS

2 tablespoons (¼ stick) butter
1½ tablespoons olive oil
2 garlic cloves, chopped
8 ounces tricolor tubular or spiral-shaped pasta,
  freshly cooked

1 7-ounce jar roasted red peppers, drained,
  chopped
½ cup grated Parmesan cheese
2 plum tomatoes, seeded, chopped
¼ cup thinly sliced fresh basil leaves

Melt butter in heavy large saucepan over medium-high heat. Add oil and garlic and stir until fragrant, about 1 minute. Mix in all remaining ingredients and toss until heated through, about 2 minutes. Season pasta to taste with salt and pepper and serve.

Steak and Corn Soft Tacos

This is a much-improved variation on the typical kid-friendly taco.

VARIATION: Dice two large boneless skinless chicken breast halves instead of steak.

4 SERVINGS

¼ cup olive oil

1 medium red onion, sliced

1 red bell pepper, sliced

1 pound round, flank or skirt steak, cut into ¼-inch-thick, long, narrow strips

1½ cups frozen whole kernel corn, cooked according to package directions, drained

½ teaspoon ground cumin

½ teaspoon chili powder

3 tablespoons minced fresh cilantro

Corn or flour tortillas

Grated cheddar cheese

Chopped fresh tomatoes

Sour cream

Heat oil in heavy large skillet over medium heat. Add onion and bell pepper and sauté until tender, about 10 minutes. Transfer to plate. Add steak to skillet and stir until no longer pink, about 1 minute. Return onion and pepper to skillet. Add corn, cumin and chili powder and stir until heated through. Season with salt and pepper. Remove from heat and mix in cilantro. Transfer to heated bowl; cover.

Cook tortillas over gas flame or electric burner until they just begin to color. Transfer to napkin lined basket. Serve tortillas, steak mixture, cheese, tomatoes and sour cream separately.

Fried-Chicken Caesar Salad

Homemade chicken nuggets will draw your kids to this salad.

VARIATION: To give this kid-friendly dish a sophisticated touch, simply add six anchovy fillets and two large garlic cloves to the dressing before processing it.

DO-AHEAD: The chicken can be prepared ahead; sauté it and toss the salad just before serving.

4 SERVINGS

½ cup olive oil

⅓ cup grated Parmesan cheese

3 tablespoons fresh lemon juice

12 chicken tenders, cut in half

⅓ cup all purpose flour

2 large eggs

1½ cups panko (Japanese breadcrumbs)* or dry breadcrumbs

⅓ cup vegetable oil

24 romaine lettuce leaves

1⅓ cups croutons

Parmesan cheese shavings

Blend first 3 ingredients in processor until smooth. Season with salt and pepper. *(Can be prepared 3 days ahead. Cover and refrigerate. Whisk to blend before using.)*

Sprinkle chicken with salt and pepper. Place flour on plate. Whisk eggs in medium bowl. Place panko in large bowl. Coat chicken with flour, dip into eggs, then coat with panko. *(Can be prepared 6 hours ahead. Cover with plastic and refrigerate.)*

Heat vegetable oil in heavy large skillet over medium-high heat. Add chicken; sauté until crisp and cooked through, about 2 minutes per side.

Toss lettuce with dressing. Arrange 6 leaves on each of 4 plates. Top with chicken. Sprinkle with croutons and Parmesan shavings and then serve.

*Panko is available in Asian markets and some supermarkets.

Potato Skins with Bacon and Cheese

Serve these with a salad from the supermarket salad bar.

VARIATION: Top with chopped sautéed sun-dried tomatoes for a vegetarian version.

3 medium russet potatoes, rinsed, dried	1 tablespoon chopped fresh parsley
Vegetable oil	¼ teaspoon cayenne pepper
5 bacon slices	¾ cup chopped green onions
1¼ cups grated sharp cheddar cheese	Sour cream
1¼ cups grated Monterey Jack cheese	

Preheat oven to 425°F. Rub potatoes with oil. Place on baking sheet. Bake potatoes until tender, about 1 hour. Cool. Maintain oven temperature. Cut each potato lengthwise into quarters. Scoop out potato flesh, leaving ½-inch-thick layer of potato on skins. Oil baking sheet. Place skins, skin side down, on sheet, spacing 1 inch apart. Sprinkle with salt and pepper.

Cook bacon in heavy large skillet over medium heat until brown and crisp. Drain. Chop bacon. Transfer to medium bowl. Add cheeses, parsley and cayenne; stir to blend. Sprinkle cheese mixture atop skins. Bake until skins are crisp and cheese melts, about 25 minutes.

Transfer skins to platter. Sprinkle with green onions; top with dollops of sour cream.

Oven-baked Drumsticks

A version of that childhood favorite—chicken legs—that adults will like, too. These are great at room temperature, so pack up the leftovers for lunch.

DO-AHEAD: Prepare the drumsticks ahead and refrigerate; bake just before serving.

12 SERVINGS

3 cups fresh breadcrumbs made from French bread	1 tablespoon dried oregano
1 cup freshly grated Parmesan cheese (about 3 ounces)	2 teaspoons salt
	1½ teaspoons pepper
6 tablespoons chopped fresh parsley	1½ cups (3 sticks) butter
4 teaspoons onion powder	9 tablespoons Dijon mustard
1 tablespoon paprika	24 chicken drumsticks

Preheat oven to 350°F. Butter 2 large baking sheets. Combine breadcrumbs, Parmesan cheese, parsley, onion powder, paprika, oregano, salt and pepper in large bowl and stir to blend. Melt butter in small saucepan over medium-low heat. Remove saucepan from heat. Add mustard and whisk to blend. Brush drumsticks generously with butter mixture, then roll in breadcrumb mixture, coating completely. Arrange on prepared sheets. *(Can be prepared 8 hours ahead. Cover and chill.)*

Bake drumsticks until cooked through, about 1 hour. Serve warm or at room temperature.

Crusty Baked Fish Sticks

These are delicious on their own, but some children (or their parents) may choose to add tartar sauce, ketchup or lemon wedges for extra flavor.

VARIATION: Try the recipe with red snapper fillets.
DO-AHEAD: The fish sticks can be prepared up to four hours ahead; bake just before serving.   6 SERVINGS

Nonstick vegetable oil spray
1 cup purchased Italian salad dressing
2 large eggs
4 cups corn bread stuffing mix
2 tablespoons finely chopped fresh parsley
All purpose flour
1½ pounds halibut fillets, cut into eighteen 4x½x1-inch pieces

Spray large rimmed baking sheet with nonstick spray. Whisk salad dressing and eggs in shallow dish to blend. Using on/off turns, process stuffing mix in processor until finely ground; transfer to another shallow dish. Mix in parsley. Place flour in another shallow dish. Dip fish sticks in flour, then in egg mixture, then in crumbs, covering completely. Place on prepared baking sheet. *(Can be prepared 4 hours ahead; refrigerate.)*

Preheat oven to 400°F. Bake fish sticks until cooked through and crispy, about 15 minutes.

FARE FOR THE FINICKY

There are certain foods that seem to appeal to all children, usually those with definable ingredients, familiar textures and little in the way of seasoning. And please—nothing too green, and no booby-trapped vegetables. And if it can be eaten out of hand with ketchup, so much the better. So how to get kids to try new things? Experiment with these tactics.

- Plant a garden with your child.
- Visit an orchard or a pick-your-own farm and encourage tasting while harvesting.
- Visit a variety of food stores, from farmers' markets to ethnic groceries to food warehouses.
- Introduce one new food a week. No one has to like it, but everyone has to try at least one bite.
- Add something new to a favorite food: bananas on a peanut butter sandwich; peas in pasta tossed with Parmesan cheese.

Real Macaroni and Cheese

A crisp, buttery crumb topping and a touch of curry make this better—by far—than the boxed variety. For those with simple tastes, reduce the amounts of curry and mustard.

VARIATION: Combine white cheddar with Gruyère cheese in place of the sharp cheddar.
DO-AHEAD: Make the macaroni and cheese a day ahead; bake just before serving.

1½ tablespoons cornstarch

1½ teaspoons dry mustard

1½ teaspoons curry powder

2¼ cups whole milk

6 tablespoons (¾ stick) butter

2¼ cups (packed) grated sharp cheddar cheese
(about 10 ounces)

8 ounces small elbow macaroni, freshly cooked

2½ cups fresh breadcrumbs made from 8 ounces
trimmed sourdough bread

Butter 8x8x2-inch glass baking dish. Combine cornstarch, 1 teaspoon dry mustard and 1 teaspoon curry powder in heavy large saucepan. Gradually whisk in milk. Add 2 tablespoons butter. Whisk over medium-high heat until sauce thickens and boils, about 1 minute. Remove from heat. Add grated cheddar cheese and whisk until smooth. Mix in macaroni. Season to taste with salt and pepper. Transfer macaroni and cheese to prepared baking dish.

Melt remaining 4 tablespoons butter in heavy large skillet over medium-high heat. Mix in remaining ½ teaspoon dry mustard and ½ teaspoon curry powder. Add fresh breadcrumbs and stir until breadcrumbs are crisp and golden, about 8 minutes.

Sprinkle breadcrumb mixture over macaroni and cheese. *(Can be prepared 1 day ahead. Cover and refrigerate.)* Preheat oven to 350°F. Bake macaroni and cheese until warmed through and bubbling at edges, about 30 minutes. Serve hot.

Ziti Casserole with Three Cheeses

This delicious take on lasagna is made with tube-shaped pasta instead of long noodles and comes together in less than an hour.

VARIATION: Try this recipe with large shells or macaroni instead.

DO-AHEAD: Prepare the dish a day ahead; bake just before serving.

---

2 tablespoons olive oil

1 onion, chopped

2 large garlic cloves, chopped

1 teaspoon fennel seeds

⅓ cup tomato paste

1 8-ounce can tomato sauce

1 cup water

1 teaspoon dried oregano, crumbled

½ teaspoon dried rubbed sage

½ cup grated Parmesan cheese

1 15-ounce container ricotta cheese

1 large egg

8 ounces mozzarella cheese, grated

12 ounces freshly cooked ziti or other tubular pasta

Heat oil in heavy large saucepan over medium-low heat. Add onion, garlic and fennel seeds and sauté until onion is translucent, about 5 minutes. Mix in tomato paste and cook 1 minute. Add tomato sauce, 1 cup water, oregano and sage. Simmer until mixture thickens slightly, stirring occasionally, about 10 minutes. Stir in ¼ cup Parmesan. Season to taste with salt and pepper. *(Can be prepared 1 day ahead. Cover tomato sauce and refrigerate.)*

Butter 9x13-inch glass baking dish. In medium bowl combine ricotta cheese and egg. Reserve ¼ cup mozzarella cheese for topping. Add remaining mozzarella to ricotta mixture and blend. Sprinkle ricotta mixture with salt and pepper.

Spread ¼ of tomato sauce over bottom of prepared dish. Layer ⅓ of pasta over. Drop half of ricotta mixture over by spoonfuls. Spread ¼ of sauce over. Repeat layering with another ⅓ of pasta, remaining ricotta mixture, ¼ of sauce and remaining pasta. Spread remaining sauce over and sprinkle with remaining ¼ cup Parmesan and reserved mozzarella. *(Can be prepared 1 day ahead. Cover and refrigerate.)* Preheat oven to 450°F. Cover casserole and bake until heated through, about 40 minutes.

Sunday Cooking for Weekday Leftovers

A couple of hours spent in the kitchen on a Sunday afternoon can yield two great meals: a big family supper that night and an easy, instant dinner (made with the leftovers) the next. Cook large.

Parsley, Sage, Rosemary and Thyme Chicken

All you need is a salad with this supper of roast chicken, potatoes and shallots. Use any leftovers in the Wild Rice and Chicken Salad (see recipe, page 162).

VARIATION: Yukon Gold or sweet potatoes can be used in place of russet potatoes; two quartered onions will replace the shallots.

---

1 4½-pound chicken

2 teaspoons dried rosemary

1½ teaspoons dried sage

1½ teaspoons dried thyme

2 bay leaves

5 tablespoons olive oil

4 small russet potatoes (unpeeled), quartered lengthwise, cut crosswise into ½-inch pieces

8 large shallots, peeled

1¾ cups (about) canned low-salt chicken broth

¼ cup balsamic vinegar or red wine vinegar

6 tablespoons (¾ stick) unsalted butter, cut into 6 pieces

Minced fresh parsley

Sprinkle chicken inside and out with salt and pepper. Combine rosemary, sage and thyme in small bowl. Rub some of mixture inside chicken. Place 1 bay leaf in cavity. Tie legs together to hold shape. Brush chicken with some of olive oil. Sprinkle with half of remaining herb mixture. Place in large baking pan. *(Can be prepared 1 day ahead. Cover and refrigerate.)* Preheat oven to 425°F. Surround chicken with potatoes and shallots. Sprinkle vegetables with remaining herb mixture and remaining olive oil. Add bay leaf to vegetables and mix well.

Bake chicken until juices run clear when chicken is pierced in thickest part of thigh and legs can be moved easily, basting chicken with pan juices and turning vegetables occasionally, about 1 hour 15 minutes. Transfer to platter. Using slotted spoon, surround with vegetables. Tent with foil.

Pour pan juices into large glass measuring cup and degrease. Add enough broth to measure 2 cups. Add vinegar to baking pan and bring to boil over medium heat, scraping up any browned bits. Boil until reduced to glaze, about 4 minutes. Add broth mixture and boil until reduced to ½ cup, about 10 minutes. Reduce heat to low and whisk in butter 1 piece at a time. Stir in minced parsley. Season sauce to taste with salt and pepper. Serve chicken with sauce.

Wild Rice and Chicken Salad

Make this salad with leftover chicken from the Parsley, Sage, Rosemary and Thyme Chicken (see recipe, page 161), or purchase a rotisserie chicken from the market.

VARIATION: Make this salad with leftover roast turkey, if you like.
DO-AHEAD: The salad can be entirely made a day ahead.

2 TO 4 SERVINGS

1 14½-ounce can low-salt chicken broth
½ cup wild rice (about 3 ounces)

2 cups diced cooked chicken
1 large celery stalk, diced
½ large crisp red apple or pear, diced
1 green onion, thinly sliced

1 tablespoon minced fresh sage or thyme or
    1 teaspoon dried
2½ tablespoons olive oil
1½ tablespoons white wine vinegar
1 teaspoon Dijon mustard
    Pinch of sugar

Combine chicken broth and wild rice in small saucepan. Bring to boil. Cover and simmer over medium-low heat until rice is tender and liquid is absorbed, about 50 minutes. Transfer to medium bowl. Cover and refrigerate until rice is well chilled.

Add chicken, celery, apple, green onion and sage to wild rice. Whisk remaining ingredients in small bowl to blend. Pour dressing over wild rice mixture and toss well. Season to taste with salt and pepper. *(Can be prepared 1 day ahead. Cover and refrigerate.)*

Meat Loaf with Barbecue Sauce

Use the leftovers in the Meat Loaf Sandwiches with Pickles (see recipe).

4 SERVINGS

1 pound lean ground beef	⅓ cup chopped fresh parsley
1½ cups fresh breadcrumbs made from French bread	½ teaspoon salt
1 cup chopped onion	½ teaspoon ground black pepper
2 large eggs	1¼ cups bottled barbecue sauce

Combine first 7 ingredients in bowl. Add ¾ cup barbecue sauce; mix until just blended. Pack mixture into 8½x4½x2½-inch metal loaf pan. *(Can be prepared 2 hours ahead. Cover with plastic and refrigerate.)* Spread remaining ½ cup barbecue sauce over top.

Preheat oven to 350°F. Bake meat loaf until top feels firm and thermometer inserted into center registers 160°F, about 1 hour 10 minutes. Let stand 15 minutes. Slice meat loaf and serve.

Meat Loaf Sandwiches with Pickles

Make these with leftovers from the Meat Loaf with Barbecue Sauce (see recipe).

VARIATION: Make your meat loaf sandwiches with any favorite breads and condiments.

2 SERVINGS

1 tablespoon butter	2 slices cooked meat loaf
4 slices sourdough bread, toasted	1 tomato, sliced
Dijon mustard	Bottled barbecue sauce
Deli-sliced dill pickles	

Butter toast. Spread 1 slice with mustard. Top with pickles, 1 slice of meat loaf and tomato slices. Drizzle with barbecue sauce. Top with second slice of toast. Repeat to make second sandwich.

Roasted Pork Loin with Garlic and Rosemary

Use any leftovers in the Tuscan Pork and Rice Salad (see recipe) or for sandwiches.

VARIATION: Use a 2½-pound boneless leg of lamb instead, if desired.

4 large garlic cloves, minced

4 teaspoons chopped fresh rosemary or
  2 teaspoons dried

1½ teaspoons coarse salt

½ teaspoon ground black pepper

1 2½-pound boneless pork loin roast, well trimmed

Fresh rosemary sprigs (optional)

Preheat oven to 400°F. Line 13x19x2-inch roasting pan with foil. Mix first 4 ingredients in bowl. Rub garlic mixture all over pork. Place pork, fat side down, in prepared roasting pan. Roast pork 30 minutes. Turn pork fat side up. Roast until thermometer inserted into center of pork loin registers 155°F, about 25 minutes longer. Remove from oven; let stand 10 minutes.

Pour any juices from roasting pan into small saucepan; set over low heat to keep warm. Cut pork crosswise into ⅓-inch-thick slices. Arrange pork slices on platter. Pour pan juices over. Garnish pork with fresh rosemary sprigs, if desired. Serve immediately.

Tuscan Pork and Rice Salad

Scrambled egg, peas and red onion enliven the recipe. Serve this salad with crusty bread.

VARIATION: If no pork is left over from the Roasted Pork Loin with Garlic and Rosemary (see recipe), broil two four-ounce boneless pork loin chops until cooked through. Diced roast chicken would be another option.

DO-AHEAD: The salad can be made up to six hours ahead.

4 SERVINGS

1 cup arborio rice or medium-grain white rice

¾ teaspoon salt

¼ cup red wine vinegar

2 tablespoons olive oil (preferably extra-virgin)

1 large egg

1 tablespoon grated Parmesan cheese

Nonstick vegetable oil spray

1 cup finely diced cooked pork

1 cup frozen petite peas, thawed

⅓ cup chopped red onion

3 tablespoons chopped fresh Italian parsley

6 large lettuce leaves

1 medium tomato, cut into thin wedges

Bring large saucepan of water to boil. Stir in rice and salt. Reduce heat to medium and simmer uncovered until rice is tender, stirring occasionally, about 15 minutes. Drain rice well. Whisk vinegar and oil in large bowl. Add warm rice and toss to coat.

Whisk egg and Parmesan cheese in small bowl to blend. Spray medium nonstick skillet with nonstick spray and heat over medium-high heat. Add egg mixture and stir constantly until scrambled, about 1 minute. Remove from heat and cool. Cut egg into small pieces. Season with pepper.

Stir egg mixture, pork, peas, red onion and parsley into rice. Season to taste with salt and pepper. *(Can be prepared 6 hours ahead. Cover and refrigerate.)* Line shallow bowl with lettuce leaves. Spoon salad onto leaves. Surround with tomato wedges. Serve salad at room temperature.

Tri-Tip with Potatoes, Carrots and Parsnips

This recipe serves up to six, but it's worth making even if you're cooking for two. Leftovers can be used in the Roast Beef and Vegetable Hash (see recipe), or for sandwiches.

VARIATION: Turnips can stand in for parsnips; rutabagas can replace the carrots.
DO-AHEAD: The meat can marinate for up to one day.

4 TO 6 SERVINGS

1 2-pound beef tri-tip roast

2 large garlic cloves, minced

1½ teaspoons dried thyme

½ cup olive oil

2 tablespoons soy sauce

3 parsnips, peeled

3 large carrots, peeled

2 russet or Yukon Gold potatoes

Place beef in large roasting pan. Rub garlic, ½ teaspoon thyme and generous amount of pepper over both sides of roast. Pour ¼ cup oil and soy sauce over roast and spoon over both sides. Turn roast fat side up. *(Can be prepared 1 day ahead. Cover and refrigerate.)*

Preheat oven to 450°F. Cut parsnips and carrots crosswise into thirds, then quarter each piece lengthwise. Halve potatoes lengthwise and crosswise, then cut each piece lengthwise into quarters. Arrange vegetables in single layer around roast (or in separate baking pan if they don't fit). Mix with remaining ¼ cup oil and 1 teaspoon thyme. Sprinkle with salt and pepper.

Place roast and vegetables in oven. Reduce temperature to 350°F and cook until thermometer inserted into thickest part of roast registers 120°F for rare, stirring vegetables occasionally, about 45 minutes. Let stand 20 minutes. Slice meat across grain. Arrange on plates. Spoon some of pan juices over. Spoon vegetables alongside and serve immediately.

Roast Beef and Vegetable Hash

This comforting and easy-to-prepare dinner is a snap with leftovers from the Tri-Tip with Potatoes, Carrots and Parsnips (see recipe).

VARIATION: The same approach to making hash can be used with virtually any leftover roast meats; try it with pork, chicken or turkey.

2 SERVINGS

2½ tablespoons olive oil

1 large onion, chopped

2 cups ½ inch pieces roasted potatoes, carrots and parsnips

2 cups ½-inch pieces roast beef

1 tablespoon soy sauce

½ teaspoon dried thyme

Minced fresh parsley

Heat oil in heavy large skillet over medium-high heat. Add onion and cook until light brown, stirring frequently, about 8 minutes. Add vegetables and stir until heated through, about 2 minutes. Add meat, soy sauce and thyme and stir just until heated through, about 2 minutes. Season to taste with salt and pepper. Sprinkle with parsley and serve immediately.

AN AFTERNOON IN THE KITCHEN

Sunday is often the time when an uninterrupted hour or two can be spent in the kitchen, planning for the week ahead. While everyone else is occupied with homework, football or weeding the garden, you can turn the afternoon into private time while you cook. Create an atmosphere for your enjoyment: Put on your favorite opera, Broadway hits or any video with Fred and Ginger. Then get busy. Here are some chores to get out of the way on Sunday, helping to ease the pressure of the busy week to come.

- Make a quart of your favorite vinaigrette; cover and refrigerate (bring to room temperature before using).
- Make marinades or dipping sauces for grilled dishes you have planned for the week; cover and refrigerate.
- Hard-boil a dozen eggs for healthy breakfasts and snacks.
- Cook polenta, pour into a buttered loaf pan and chill. Broil, grill or sauté to serve during the week.
- Make meatballs and freeze.
- Soak dried beans.
- Roast and peel red bell peppers.
- Steam rice (reheat in the microwave).
- Make homemade fudge sauce for ice cream.

Sage-roasted Turkey
with Caramelized Onions

Make this turkey on a Sunday afternoon for a delicious family supper, and use leftovers in the Turkey Enchiladas (see recipe) or in sandwiches during the week.

10 TO 12
SERVINGS

1½ pounds onions, sliced

3 tablespoons vegetable oil

1 14- to 15-pound turkey; neck, heart and gizzard cut into 1-inch pieces and reserved

2 tablespoons (¼ stick) butter, room temperature

8 fresh sage leaves plus 1½ teaspoons chopped

1 cup (or more) canned low-salt chicken broth

6 tablespoons all purpose flour

¾ cup dry white wine

Pinch of ground nutmeg

Position rack in bottom third of oven and preheat to 425°F. Toss onions and 2 tablespoons oil in large roasting pan. Roast onions until golden brown, stirring every 15 minutes, about 1 hour.

Meanwhile, rinse turkey inside and out; pat dry. Slide hand under skin of turkey breast to loosen skin. Spread butter under skin over breast meat. Arrange 4 sage leaves under skin on each side of breast. Tuck wing tips under turkey; tie legs together loosely. Rub turkey all over with 1 tablespoon vegetable oil; sprinkle turkey with salt and pepper.

Place turkey atop onions in pan. Add neck, heart and gizzard pieces to pan. Roast turkey 30 minutes. Pour 1 cup chicken broth into pan. Tent turkey loosely with foil. Reduce oven temperature to 325°F. Roast turkey 2 hours. Uncover; continue to roast until turkey is golden brown and thermometer inserted into thickest part of thigh registers 180°F, basting occasionally with pan juices, about 1 hour longer. Transfer to platter. Tent loosely with foil; let stand 30 minutes.

Remove neck and giblet pieces from pan; discard. Pour onion mixture into large glass measuring cup; spoon off fat, reserving 2 tablespoons. Add enough chicken broth to onion mixture in measuring cup if necessary to measure 5 cups total.

Heat 2 tablespoons turkey fat in large saucepan over medium-high heat. Add 1½ teaspoons chopped sage; stir 30 seconds. Add flour; whisk until beginning to color, about 3 minutes (mixture will be dry and crumbly). Gradually whisk in onion mixture, wine and nutmeg. Simmer until gravy thickens, whisking 5 minutes; season with salt and pepper. Carve turkey; serve hot with gravy.

Turkey Enchiladas

These easy enchiladas can be prepared with leftovers from the Sage-roasted Turkey with Caramelized Onions (see recipe).

VARIATION: This can also be made with roast chicken.

DO-AHEAD: Prepare the sauce three days ahead and the enchiladas a day ahead.

---

3 tablespoons plus ½ cup vegetable oil

1¾ cups finely chopped onions

1 28-ounce can enchilada sauce

5 plum tomatoes, finely chopped

1½ teaspoons finely chopped canned
chipotle chilies*

1 cup chopped fresh cilantro

3 cups coarsely shredded cooked turkey

2 cups grated Monterey Jack cheese

¾ cup sour cream

12 5- to 6-inch corn tortillas

6 SERVINGS

Heat 3 tablespoons oil in large saucepan over medium heat. Add 1½ cups onions and sauté until tender, about 5 minutes. Add enchilada sauce, tomatoes and chipotle chilies. Cover; simmer 20 minutes, stirring often. Remove from heat. Stir in ½ cup cilantro. Season sauce with salt and pepper. *(Can be prepared 3 days ahead. Cover with plastic and refrigerate.)*

Mix turkey, 1½ cups cheese, sour cream, remaining ¼ cup onions and ½ cup cilantro in large bowl. Season turkey mixture to taste with salt and pepper.

Preheat oven to 350°F. Heat ½ cup oil in medium skillet over medium heat. Cook 1 tortilla until pliable, about 20 seconds per side. Drain on paper towels. Repeat with remaining tortillas.

Spread ½ cup sauce in 13x9x2-inch glass baking dish. Spoon ¼ cup turkey mixture in center of each tortilla. Roll up tortillas. Arrange seam side down in dish. Spoon 2½ cups sauce over enchiladas. Sprinkle with remaining ½ cup cheese. Bake enchiladas until heated through, about 30 minutes. *(Can be prepared 1 day ahead. Cool, cover and refrigerate. Rewarm in 350°F oven until heated through.)*

Rewarm remaining sauce in saucepan over medium-low heat. Transfer to sauceboat. Serve enchiladas, passing remaining sauce separately.

*Chipotle chilies canned in a spicy tomato sauce, sometimes called adobo, are sold at Latin American markets, specialty foods stores and some supermarkets.

Roast Leg of Lamb with Olive and Rosemary Paste

Save leftovers (which will keep for a couple of days) to use in the Roast Lamb and Arugula Sandwiches with Spicy Tomato Jam (see recipe).

DO-AHEAD: The olive and rosemary paste can be prepared up to four days ahead, and the lamb takes less than an hour to roast.

8 SERVINGS

1 cup Kalamata olives or other brine-cured
  black olives, pitted

3 large garlic cloves

1 tablespoon chopped fresh rosemary or
  1 teaspoon dried

¼ cup olive oil

1 4½-pound boneless leg of lamb

Using on/off turns, blend olives, garlic and rosemary in processor until chopped. Gradually add oil, blending until coarse paste forms. Season paste with salt and pepper. *(Can be prepared 4 days ahead. Cover and refrigerate.)* Sprinkle lamb with salt and pepper. Place lamb, boned side up, on rimmed baking sheet. Spread olive paste over top of lamb.

Preheat oven to 350°F. Roast lamb 30 minutes. Increase oven temperature to 400°F. Continue roasting until thermometer inserted into thickest part of lamb registers 135°F for medium-rare, about 20 minutes. Let lamb stand 15 minutes before carving.

Roast Lamb and Arugula Sandwiches with Spicy Tomato Jam

Use leftovers from the Roast Leg of Lamb with Olive and Rosemary Paste (see recipe) to make these sophisticated sandwiches.

VARIATION: The jalapeño is optional; use basil, oregano or rosemary in place of cilantro.
DO-AHEAD: Make the spicy jam up to two days ahead of time; putting the sandwiches together takes almost no time at all.

Spicy Tomato Jam (see recipe)

8 5x4-inch rectangles ciabatta (cut from 2 ciabatta loaves),* or focaccia, halved horizontally

8 ½-inch-thick slices roast lamb

5 cups arugula

Spread tomato jam over cut sides of bread. Arrange lamb and arugula over bottom of each bread, dividing equally. Cover with bread tops and then serve.

*A rustic, chewy, oval-shaped Italian flatbread available at many bakeries and supermarkets.

Spicy Tomato Jam

¼ cup olive oil

3 cups chopped onions

6 garlic cloves, minced

2 tablespoons minced jalapeño chili

3½ pounds tomatoes, seeded, chopped

6 tablespoons red wine vinegar

1½ tablespoons sugar

½ cup chopped fresh cilantro

Heat oil in heavy large pot over medium heat. Add onions and sauté until softened, about 8 minutes. Add garlic and jalapeño, sauté 4 minutes. Add tomatoes, vinegar and sugar; cook until almost dry, stirring frequently, about 40 minutes. Mix in cilantro. Season to taste with salt and pepper. Cool. *(Can be prepared 2 days ahead. Cover and refrigerate.)*

Every-Night Extras

There is dinner to cook almost every night, but there are also lunches to make for the next day and weekday birthdays to celebrate. Then there are the cravings before and after dinner, whether for a snack to tame your hunger or for something sweet later. This section covers these bases—and more.

While you can always reach for a handful of pretzels, a snack can sometimes be more interesting, time and energy permitting. The seven recipes in "Fast Snacks" don't take much effort, but they pack a lot of flavor. After dinner, you may turn straight to lunch—packing one for tomorrow—or you may find yourself in the mood for dessert, and we don't just mean a piece of fruit. "Lunch-Box Treats" includes recipes for special finds for the brown-bag set, and "Quick and Sweet" offers seven recipes for delicious yet simple desserts.

And when the occasion can't wait until the weekend, look to "Special Nights" for main-course-and-dessert menus that guarantee a festive celebration even during the week.

Fast Snacks

Sometimes the hardest thing about making dinner is waiting for dinner when you're hungry at the end of the day. Here are seven fast and simple snacks—more interesting than cheese and crackers—to help you hold out for that delicious meal still in the oven.

Braised Kale Crostini

This Italian-style appetizer is great with a glass of red wine.

VARIATION: Use beet greens instead of kale.

DO-AHEAD: Note that the toasts and braised kale can be prepared a day ahead.

---

12 ½-inch-thick Italian bread slices (each slice about 2x3 inches)

8 tablespoons olive oil

5 large garlic cloves, 1 halved and 4 minced

½ teaspoon dried crushed red pepper

1 pound kale, thick ribs and stems cut away, leaves sliced

3½ cups canned low-salt chicken broth

Preheat oven to 375°F. Brush bread slices with 2 tablespoons olive oil; arrange bread on baking sheet. Bake until beginning to color, about 6 minutes. Rub toasts with halved garlic.

Heat 4 tablespoons olive oil in heavy large pot over medium-high heat. Add minced garlic and dried red pepper and stir 30 seconds. Add kale and broth and bring to boil. Reduce heat, cover and simmer 15 minutes. Uncover and continue to simmer until kale is tender and broth has evaporated, stirring often, about 15 minutes. Season to taste with salt and pepper. *(Can be prepared 1 day ahead. Store toasts in airtight container. Cover kale mixture and refrigerate. Rewarm kale over medium heat, stirring frequently, until heated through.)* Top toasts with kale. Drizzle toasts with remaining 2 tablespoons olive oil and then serve.

Herb and Lemon Goat Cheese Spread

This tangy spread is delicious with crackers or a crudité mix of celery sticks, red bell pepper strips and Belgian endive leaves.

DO-AHEAD: Make this spread a day ahead, but let it stand for an hour before serving.

5 ounces (about ½ cup) soft fresh goat cheese, room temperature

2 teaspoons chopped fresh thyme

2 teaspoons grated lemon peel

1 garlic clove, minced

5 teaspoons olive oil

16 French-bread baguette slices, toasted

Place goat cheese in small bowl. Mix thyme, lemon peel and garlic in another small bowl; season with ground black pepper. Mix half of thyme mixture into goat cheese. Add olive oil to remaining half of thyme mixture. Form cheese into 2½-inch round; flatten slightly. Place in center of plate. *(Can be prepared 1 day ahead. Cover and refrigerate goat cheese mixture and oil mixture separately. Let both stand at room temperature 1 hour before continuing.)*

Spoon oil-thyme mixture over top of cheese. Surround cheese with baguette slices and serve.

Sugar and Spice Pepitas

Pepitas are pumpkin seeds. They're tossed with sweet and hot seasonings, then baked, in this 15-minute snack. Have a handful with an ice-cold beer.

VARIATION: Try making this with raw almonds instead of pepitas for a change.
DO-AHEAD: These keep at room temperature for up to three days.

MAKES 2 CUPS

Nonstick vegetable oil spray

2 cups shelled pepitas

⅓ cup sugar

1 large egg white, beaten until frothy

1 tablespoon chili powder

1 teaspoon ground cinnamon

½ teaspoon salt

¼ teaspoon ground cumin

¼ to ½ teaspoon cayenne pepper

Preheat oven to 350°F. Spray baking sheet with nonstick spray. Mix pepitas and next 6 ingredients in medium bowl. Stir in ¼ teaspoon to ½ teaspoon cayenne pepper, depending on spiciness desired. Spread pepitas in single layer on prepared baking sheet.

Bake pepitas until golden and dry, stirring occasionally, about 15 minutes. Remove from oven. Separate pepitas with fork while still warm. Cool. _(Can be prepared 3 days ahead. Store in airtight container at room temperature.)_

QUICK EATS

At the end of a long day, it can be a long, hungry wait for dinner. Here are some ideas for quick snacks that will take the edge off an appetite without ruining the meal to come.

- Carrot, jicama and celery sticks with ranch dressing.
- Fresh radishes with coarse salt for dipping.
- Cherry tomatoes with blue cheese dressing.
- Miniature rice cakes spread with purchased hummus.
- Toasted pita triangles spread with _taramasalata_.
- Bagel chips spread with roasted red pepper puree (easily made with peppers from a jar) and crumbled goat cheese.
- Guacamole with red bell pepper strips.
- Fresh tomato salsa with green bell pepper strips.
- Fresh fennel strips with Caesar dressing.
- Cooked green beans with green goddess dressing.
- Miniature bagels split, brushed with tomato sauce, topped with mozzarella cheese and broiled.

Caesar Dip with Crudités

This dip has all the appealing flavors of Caesar salad; small romaine lettuce leaves and assorted fresh vegetables make great dippers.

8 TO 10
SERVINGS

1 cup mayonnaise

½ cup sour cream

½ cup freshly grated Parmesan cheese

1 tablespoon fresh lemon juice

1 garlic clove, pressed

1 anchovy fillet, mashed

Small romaine leaves

Assorted fresh vegetables

Whisk first 6 ingredients in small bowl to blend. Season dip with salt and pepper. *(Can be prepared 1 day ahead. Cover with plastic wrap and refrigerate.)* Serve with lettuce and vegetables.

Italian Salami and Cheese Toasts

These taste like crispy little pizzas, and take just minutes to make.

2 SERVINGS

6 ½-inch-thick diagonally cut French bread
    baguette slices

    Olive oil

1 garlic clove, halved

6 thin slices Italian dry salami

6 slices provolone cheese

    Dried oregano

6 Italian parsley leaves

Preheat broiler. Broil one side of bread slices until toasted. Brush second side of each with oil, rub lightly with garlic, then sprinkle with pepper. Broil second side until toasted. Top with salami and cheese, folding cheese under to fit. Sprinkle with oregano. Broil until cheese melts. Top with parsley.

Spicy Guacamole

A truly authentic, utterly simple take on the classic.

MAKES ABOUT
1 CUP

1 large ripe avocado, peeled, pitted

2 teaspoons fresh lime juice

½ cup chopped fresh cilantro

¼ cup finely chopped onion

2 large garlic cloves, finely chopped

2 large serrano chilies, seeded, chopped

¼ teaspoon salt

Using fork, mash avocado with lime juice in small bowl. Add cilantro, chopped onion, chopped garlic, serrano chilies and salt and stir to combine.

Vegetables with Red Pepper and Garlic Mayonnaise

This is a simplified version of *rouille,* the garlic sauce that accompanies French fish soups.

MAKES ABOUT
1 CUP

2 large garlic cloves

½ cup diced drained roasted red peppers from jar

½ teaspoon red wine vinegar

¼ teaspoon cayenne pepper

½ cup mayonnaise

Assorted raw vegetables

With processor running, drop garlic through feed tube and mince. Scrape down sides of bowl. Add roasted peppers, vinegar and cayenne and process until mixture is almost smooth. Add ¼ cup mayonnaise and process using on/off turns just until combined. Transfer sauce to small bowl; mix in remaining ¼ cup mayonnaise. Season to taste with salt and pepper. Cover and refrigerate at least 30 minutes and up to 1 day. Serve with vegetables for dipping.

Lunch-Box Treats

For many parents, dinner segues into lunch as they move from the table to the kitchen to pack tomorrow's brown bags. Few things are more appreciated by kids than a special treat in their lunch box. Here are five ideas for quick-cooking goodies that will turn any lunch into a feast.

Peanut Butter and Chocolate Chip Cookies

Two old-fashioned flavors—peanut butter and chocolate chips—team up in these irresistible cookies. The simple dough has no flour in it.

VARIATION: M&M's or Reese's Pieces can replace the chocolate chips.
DO-AHEAD: These keep well in an airtight container at room temperature.

1 cup super chunky peanut butter

1 cup (packed) golden brown sugar

1 large egg

1 teaspoon baking soda

½ teaspoon vanilla extract

1 cup miniature semisweet chocolate chips
(about 6 ounces)

MAKES ABOUT 24

Preheat oven to 350°F. Mix first 5 ingredients in medium bowl. Stir in chocolate chips. Using moistened hands, form generous 1 tablespoon dough into ball for each cookie. Arrange on 2 ungreased baking sheets, spacing about 2 inches apart.

Bake cookies until puffed, golden on bottom and still soft to touch in center, about 12 minutes. Cool on sheets 5 minutes. Transfer to racks; cool completely. *(Can be prepared 3 days ahead. Store in airtight container at room temperature.)*

Banana-Cinnamon Snacking Cake

Yogurt makes this cake moist and light. It would also be good for breakfast.

VARIATION: For a richer version of this cake, use sour cream instead of yogurt and add one cup finely chopped toasted walnuts.

DO-AHEAD: This cake can be prepared a day ahead.

8 SERVINGS

Nonstick vegetable oil spray

1½ cups all purpose flour

½ cup sugar

2 teaspoons baking powder

1 teaspoon baking soda

1 teaspoon ground cinnamon

½ teaspoon salt

1 cup plain yogurt

¾ cup mashed ripe banana

2 tablespoons vegetable oil

1 large egg

1 teaspoon vanilla extract

Powdered sugar

Preheat oven to 400°F. Spray 9-inch square baking pan with nonstick spray. Combine flour, sugar, baking powder, baking soda, cinnamon and salt in large bowl. Whisk together yogurt, mashed banana, vegetable oil, egg and vanilla in medium bowl. Pour over dry ingredients and stir gently until just blended; do not overmix. Spread batter in prepared pan. Bake cake until top is light brown and edges begin to pull away from sides of pan, about 20 minutes.

Cool cake in pan on rack 10 minutes. Loosen sides of cake with spatula and turn out onto rack. Invert cake right side up and cool completely. Transfer to plate. Sprinkle lightly with powdered sugar. *(Can be prepared 1 day ahead. Cover with plastic wrap and store at room temperature.)*

Chocolate Mint Cupcakes

These easy cupcakes are ideal for a child's birthday celebration at school or any kid-filled party. Decorate them according to occasion or holiday, varying the food coloring in the frosting, and topping with everything from chopped candies to shaped sprinkles.

VARIATION: For adult-friendly cupcakes, use almond extract in place of the peppermint extract, omit the green food coloring and garnish with slivered toasted almonds.
DO-AHEAD: Make these up to two days ahead.

CUPCAKES

1 box devil's food cake mix (1 pound 2.25 ounces)

1⅓ cups water

½ cup vegetable oil

3 large eggs

1 tablespoon vanilla extract

1½ cups semisweet chocolate chips

FROSTING

12 ounces cream cheese, room temperature

¼ cup (½ stick) unsalted butter, room temperature

1¾ cups powdered sugar

½ teaspoon peppermint extract

2 drops green food coloring

FOR CUPCAKES: Preheat oven to 350°F. Line eighteen ⅓-cup muffin cups with muffin papers. Combine first 5 ingredients in large bowl. Using electric mixer, beat 2 minutes. Mix in chocolate chips. Pour batter into cups. Bake until tester inserted into center comes out with crumbs attached, about 25 minutes. Cool cupcakes completely on racks.
FOR FROSTING: Using electric mixer, beat all ingredients in medium bowl until light and fluffy. Spread frosting over cupcakes and decorate as desired. *(Can be made 2 days ahead; cover and chill.)*

Oatmeal Bars with Chocolate Chunks

These bar cookies are sure to become a lunch-box favorite.

VARIATION: Add raisins if desired; try walnuts instead of pecans for a change, or omit the nuts entirely for kids who don't like them.

DO-AHEAD: Make these up to a day ahead of time.

MAKES ABOUT
3 DOZEN

2 cups all purpose flour

1 cup quick-cooking oats

1 tablespoon baking powder

¾ teaspoon salt

1 cup (2 sticks) unsalted butter, room temperature

1¼ cups sugar

1¼ cups (packed) golden brown sugar

2 large eggs

⅔ cup mashed ripe bananas (about 2 large)

2 teaspoons vanilla extract

6 ounces semisweet chocolate, cut into chunks

1 cup pecans, toasted, chopped

Preheat oven to 350°F. Butter and flour 15x10x1-inch baking sheet. Blend first 4 ingredients in medium bowl. Beat butter in large bowl until fluffy. Add both sugars and beat until well blended. Add eggs 1 at a time, beating well after each addition. Beat in mashed bananas, then vanilla. Stir in flour mixture, then chopped chocolate and pecans.

Spread batter in prepared pan. Bake until tester inserted into center comes out clean and top is golden, about 45 minutes. Cool in pan on rack. Cut into 3x2-inch bars and serve. *(Can be prepared 1 day ahead. Store in airtight container at room temperature.)*

Almond-Raisin Granola

This makes a great lunchtime treat; it's also delicious over ice cream or frozen yogurt.

VARIATION: Add chocolate chips to the granola after it has cooled, if desired.

DO-AHEAD: Note that this granola keeps well in an airtight container; make a batch on the weekend and enjoy it all week.

8 SERVINGS

Nonstick vegetable oil spray

3 cups old-fashioned oats

1 cup slivered almonds

¾ cup shredded sweetened coconut

⅓ cup sesame seeds

6 tablespoons pure maple syrup

6 tablespoons (packed) dark brown sugar

¼ cup vegetable oil

2 tablespoons warm water

½ teaspoon salt

1 cup golden raisins

Preheat oven to 250°F. Lightly spray rimmed baking sheet with nonstick spray. Toss oats and next 3 ingredients in large bowl. Whisk syrup, brown sugar, oil, 2 tablespoons warm water and salt in small bowl to blend. Pour syrup mixture over oat mixture and stir to combine. Transfer to prepared baking sheet. Bake until evenly browned, stirring occasionally, about 1 hour 15 minutes. Cool. Transfer to large bowl. Mix in raisins. *(Can be made 1 week ahead. Store in airtight container at room temperature.)*

BEYOND THE SANDWICH

When lunch is always a PB&J or ham and cheese, why not break out of the (lunch) box and try something different?

- A bran muffin split and spread with crunchy peanut butter.
- Chunks of mild cheddar cheese and tart Granny Smith apples.
- Leftover pizza (It will come to room temperature by lunchtime).
- A whole wheat bagel with cream cheese, cut into quarters.
- A corn muffin split and filled with slices of Monterey Jack cheese.
- Leftover meat loaf in a French roll.
- Leftover pasta mixed with chopped tomato, black olives and chunks of mozzarella cheese.
- Fruit salad and yogurt.
- Canned tuna mixed with chopped celery and mayonnaise and sandwiched between melba toasts.

Quick and Sweet

Sometimes dinner isn't dinner until it ends in something sweet. For those nights, these practically instant desserts, made with ingredients you very likely have on hand, will fill the bill.

Vanilla Peach Pie

This pie is as easy as sweetened fresh fruit sandwiched between two ready-made pie crusts. It does take a while to bake, though, so you may want to make it on Sunday afternoon to enjoy during the week. It's great on its own or with vanilla ice cream.

VARIATION: Nectarines or juicy pears would work in place of peaches.
DO-AHEAD: Prepare this pie up to a day ahead.

4 pounds ripe peaches, peeled, halved, pitted, each half cut into 6 wedges (about 8 cups)

½ cup plus 1 tablespoon sugar

¼ cup (packed) golden brown sugar

¼ cup all purpose flour

¼ teaspoon ground cardamom

1 vanilla bean, split lengthwise

1 15-ounce package refrigerated pie crusts (2 crusts)

Whipping cream (for glaze)

Position rack in bottom third of oven and preheat to 400°F. Combine peaches, ½ cup sugar, brown sugar, flour and cardamom in large bowl. Scrape in seeds from vanilla bean; discard bean. Toss to blend well. Let stand until dry ingredients are moistened, about 15 minutes.

Roll out 1 pie crust on lightly floured surface to 12½-inch round. Transfer to 9-inch-diameter glass pie dish. Trim overhang to ½ inch. Spoon peach filling into crust, mounding slightly in center. Roll out second pie crust to 12-inch round. Drape crust over peach filling. Trim overhang to ¾ inch. Fold edge of top and bottom crusts under, pressing to seal. Crimp edges decoratively. Cut 4 slits in top crust to allow steam to escape during baking. Brush crust lightly with whipping cream. Sprinkle top of crust with remaining 1 tablespoon sugar.

Place pie on baking sheet. Bake 45 minutes. Cover crust edges with foil to prevent overbrowning. Continue to bake until crust is golden and juices bubble thickly, about 1 hour longer. Cool completely on rack. *(Can be prepared 1 day ahead. Cover loosely with foil and store at room temperature.)*

Quick and Easy Spice Cake

Slices of leftover spice cake make a great breakfast treat.

VARIATION: Add currants to the batter for something different. A mix of one teaspoon cinnamon, half a teaspoon nutmeg, a quarter-teaspoon ginger and a quarter-teaspoon cloves could stand in for the pumpkin pie spice if you don't have that handy.

8 SERVINGS

2½ cups all purpose flour

2 teaspoons pumpkin pie spice

1½ teaspoons baking soda

½ teaspoon salt

1¼ cups (packed) dark brown sugar

½ cup (1 stick) unsalted butter, melted, cooled

1 large egg

1 cup buttermilk

1 cup chopped walnuts

Rum raisin or vanilla ice cream (optional)

Preheat oven to 350°F. Butter and flour 8-inch square metal baking pan. Mix first 4 ingredients in medium bowl to blend. Whisk sugar, butter and egg in large bowl until smooth. Whisk in dry ingredients alternately with buttermilk, beginning with dry ingredients. Fold in nuts. Transfer batter to prepared pan. Bake until tester inserted into center comes out clean, about 1 hour. Cool cake slightly in pan on rack. Slice and serve warm with ice cream, if desired. *(Can be prepared 1 day ahead.)*

Plum-Nectarine Crisp

This is delicious on its own or served with vanilla ice cream or whipped cream.

VARIATION: Fresh peaches would also work well in this crisp.

4 SERVINGS

1 pound plums, pitted, sliced

1 pound nectarines, pitted, sliced

¼ cup plus ⅓ cup (packed) brown sugar

½ teaspoon ground cinnamon

½ cup old-fashioned oats

⅓ cup all purpose flour

Pinch of salt

5 tablespoons unsalted butter, room temperature

Preheat oven to 375°F. Mix fruit, ¼ cup sugar and ¼ teaspoon cinnamon in medium bowl. Transfer to 9-inch-diameter pie dish. Combine oats, ⅓ cup sugar, ¼ teaspoon cinnamon, flour and salt in processor. Add butter and cut in, using on/off turns, until mixture is crumbly. Sprinkle over fruit. Bake until dessert is bubbly, about 45 minutes. Serve hot, warm or at room temperature.

Lemon Cream Tartlets

Purchased lemon curd (found with the jams and jellies at many supermarkets) and frozen puff-pastry shells make this dessert very easy.

VARIATION: Layer the lemon cream with thinly sliced purchased pound cake in two wine-glasses and garnish with strawberries for an easy trifle.
DO-AHEAD: Prepare the filling ahead, but fill the tartlet shells just before serving.

½ cup purchased lemon curd

3½ teaspoons fresh lemon juice

1½ teaspoons grated lemon peel

¼ cup chilled whipping cream

2 frozen puff-pastry shells, baked according to package instructions

2 SERVINGS

Combine lemon curd, lemon juice and lemon peel in medium bowl and whisk until smooth. Beat cream in small bowl until stiff peaks form. Fold whipped cream into lemon mixture. *(Filling can be prepared up to 1 day ahead. Cover tightly and refrigerate.)*

Spoon lemon cream into puff-pastry shells, dividing equally, and serve.

Candy Crunch Ice Cream

Chopped candy turns plain ice cream into a wonderfully easy weeknight dessert.

VARIATION: Use your favorite ice cream and candy combinations to tailor this recipe to your tastes—vanilla ice cream with chopped peanut butter cup candies or chocolate chip ice cream with halved Junior Mints would both be delicious.
DO-AHEAD: Mix a big batch and keep this ice cream on hand all week. Or not.

2 TO 4 SERVINGS

1 pint coffee ice cream, slightly softened

2½ ounces Cadbury's Fruit & Nut bar, coarsely chopped

2 tablespoons dark rum (optional)

2 teaspoons instant espresso powder

Mix ice cream, candy, rum (if desired) and espresso powder in large bowl. Transfer to covered container and freeze until firm. *(Can be prepared 1 week ahead. Keep frozen.)*

Strawberries with Milk Chocolate Fondue

Chocolate-covered strawberries were the inspiration for this easy dessert fondue.

VARIATION: Serve the fondue with banana slices and angel food cake or pound cake slices.

2 SERVINGS

1 3-ounce good-quality milk chocolate bar (such as Lindt), chopped

2 tablespoons half and half

1 tablespoon crème de cassis (black-currant-flavored liqueur), cassis syrup or brandy (optional)

1 pint strawberries

Melt chocolate with half and half in heavy small saucepan over low heat, stirring until smooth. Mix in crème de cassis, if desired. Pour into heated bowl. Serve, passing berries to dip into chocolate.

Apple and Pear Sauté

This simple fruit sauté is a satisfying dessert served with ice cream.

VARIATION: Top with lightly sweetened mascarpone cheese as an alternative to ice cream.   4 SERVINGS

---

2 tablespoons unsalted butter

2 large Golden Delicious apples, cored, cut into
   ¾-inch-thick slices

4 small Bosc pears, cored, cut into
   ¾-inch-thick slices

½ teaspoon ground allspice

½ teaspoon finely grated lemon peel
   Vanilla, butter-pecan or dulce de leche
   ice cream

Melt butter in heavy large skillet over medium-high heat. Add apples and stir 2 minutes. Add pears and stir 2 minutes. Add allspice and lemon peel and sauté until fruit is just tender, about 2 minutes. Serve over ice cream.

PANTRY DESSERTS

When a handful of walnuts and a pear just doesn't cut it for dessert, consider some of the following treats made with foods you may well have in the refrigerator or freezer, or on the pantry shelf.

- Toasted pound cake with fresh berries.
- Vanilla ice cream topped with warmed fruit preserves.
- Applesauce mixed with cinnamon and brown sugar, then swirled into vanilla yogurt.
- Toasted waffles topped with frozen yogurt.
- Blueberries mixed with vanilla yogurt and sprinkled with maple sugar and chopped walnuts.
- Fresh raspberries or blackberries splashed with orange juice.
- Orange wedges drizzled with sweet Muscat wine.
- Pear slices sautéed in butter and sprinkled with sugar, served warm with chocolate or caramel sauce.
- Sliced peaches topped with crushed amaretto cookies.
- Chocolate or coffee ice cream topped with coffee liqueur.
- Strawberries drizzled with balsamic vinegar, served with a bowl of powdered sugar for dipping.
- Sliced nectarines splashed with red wine that has been sweetened slightly with sugar.

Special Nights

What to do when a birthday, an anniversary or another special occasion falls during the week? You could go out, but a home-cooked meal might be the best gift of all. How about a memorable (yet easy) main course and a sumptuous (yet easy) dessert?

Cornish Hens with Orange-Teriyaki Sauce

Serve the Pound Cake with Ice Cream and Cider Sauce (see recipe) for dessert.

4 SERVINGS

1 cup thick teriyaki baste and glaze

1 cup orange juice

4 green onions, finely chopped

2 tablespoons grated orange peel

1 tablespoon minced peeled fresh ginger

4 1- to 1¼-pound Cornish game hens

⅔ cup canned low-salt chicken broth

Whisk first 5 ingredients in bowl to blend for marinade. Place hens in plastic bag. Add 1 cup marinade; seal bag. Let marinate 1 hour or refrigerate overnight. Reserve remaining marinade.

Preheat oven to 400°F. Place rack on rimmed baking sheet. Arrange hens on rack; drizzle with marinade from bag. Roast hens until cooked through, basting occasionally with reserved marinade, about 1 hour. Transfer hens to platter. Scrape juices into saucepan; add broth and any remaining marinade. Bring sauce to boil. Season with salt and pepper; spoon over hens.

Pound Cake with Ice Cream and Cider Sauce

4 SERVINGS

3 cups apple cider

1 cup whipping cream

2 tablespoons (¼ stick) chilled unsalted butter, cut into small pieces

¼ teaspoon vanilla extract

2 drops lemon extract

4 slices purchased pound cake

1 pint vanilla ice cream

½ cup walnuts, toasted, chopped

Boil cider in large skillet until reduced to ½ cup, about 18 minutes. Add cream; boil until slightly thickened, 2 minutes. Transfer to bowl. Whisk in butter and both extracts. Cool slightly, then chill until cold, at least 1 hour. Place 1 slice of cake on each plate. Top each with ice cream, sauce and nuts.

Pan-braised Chicken with Dried Fruits and Olives

Serve this with couscous or rice and steamed carrots tossed with chopped fresh mint. Finish off the meal with the Fudgy Chocolate Birthday cake (see recipe). The chicken recipe doubles easily for a big celebration.

DO-AHEAD: The entire dish can be made a day ahead and rewarmed just before serving.

4 SERVINGS

4 skinless boneless chicken breast halves

2 teaspoons ground cumin

¼ cup olive oil

4 garlic cloves, finely chopped

1½ cups mixed dried fruits (about 6 ounces), large pieces halved

1 cup dry white wine

1 cup canned low-salt chicken broth

16 brine-cured cracked green olives (about 4 ounces)

Sprinkle chicken on all sides with cumin, salt and pepper. Heat oil in heavy large skillet over medium heat. Add chicken and sauté until brown, about 2 minutes per side. Push chicken to side of skillet. Add garlic to skillet and stir 30 seconds. Add dried fruits, wine, broth and olives and bring to boil. Simmer chicken uncovered until just cooked through, turning chicken occasionally with tongs, about 10 minutes. Transfer chicken to ovenproof serving bowl. Increase heat and boil sauce until slightly thickened, about 6 minutes. Spoon sauce over chicken. *(Can be prepared 1 day ahead. Cool, then cover with foil and refrigerate. Rewarm, covered, in 350°F oven, stirring occasionally, until chicken is heated through, about 20 minutes.)* Serve warm.

Fudgy Chocolate Birthday Cake

Sour cream and vegetable oil moisten this cake-mix cake, and raspberry jam adds a nice touch to the frosting. Decorate the cake with edible flowers and candles.

DO-AHEAD: The cake layers can be baked up to a week ahead of time and frozen, and the whole cake can be made a day ahead.

1 box devil's food cake mix (1 pound 2.25 ounces)

1 cup water

⅓ cup vegetable oil

3 large eggs

1 teaspoon vanilla extract

1 cup sour cream

2 12-ounce packages semisweet chocolate chips (4 cups)

½ cup seedless raspberry jam

3 tablespoons unsalted butter

2 cups powdered sugar

Position rack in center of oven and preheat to 350°F. Butter three 8-inch-diameter nonstick cake pans with 1½-inch-high sides. Place cake mix, 1 cup water, oil, eggs, vanilla and ¼ cup sour cream in large bowl. Using electric mixer, beat batter 2 minutes. Stir in 1 cup chocolate chips.

Divide batter among prepared pans (about 1¾ cups batter for each). Bake until tester inserted into center of cake layers comes out clean, about 25 minutes. Cool cake layers in pans on racks 15 minutes. Run small sharp knife between pan sides and cake layers to loosen. Turn out onto racks; cool completely. *(Can be prepared ahead. Wrap in plastic and let stand at room temperature 1 day or freeze 1 week. Thaw at room temperature before continuing.)*

Bring ½ cup raspberry jam and 3 tablespoons unsalted butter to simmer in heavy large saucepan over medium heat, stirring often. Remove from heat. Add remaining 3 cups semisweet chocolate chips and stir until melted. Add remaining ¾ cup sour cream and 2 cups powdered sugar. Using electric mixer, beat frosting in pan until smooth and thick, about 2 minutes.

Place 1 cake layer on platter. Spread ¾ cup frosting over. Top with second cake layer. Spread ¾ cup frosting over. Top with third cake layer. Chill cake until frosting sets slightly, about 15 minutes. Spread remaining frosting in swirls over top and sides of cake. *(Can be prepared 1 day ahead. Cover with cake dome and let stand at room temperature.)*

Roast Rack of Lamb with Madeira-Peppercorn Sauce

Toss a salad of endive, watercress and pear with a blue cheese vinaigrette to start. Serve the lamb with a potato gratin and *haricots verts.* **The Warm Cinnamon-Apple Tart with Currants (see recipe) makes a perfect ending to a special meal.**

VARIATION: This sauce would also work with thick pork chops (with bones); make sure they reach an internal temperature of 150°F for food safety.

DO-AHEAD: Note that the sauce and lamb can be prepared eight hours ahead. The lamb needs to roast for just 30 minutes before serving.

4 SERVINGS

6 medium shallots

4 tablespoons (½ stick) chilled unsalted butter

1¼ cups Madeira

1 tablespoon drained green peppercorns in brine, coarsely chopped

2 1¼-pound racks of lamb, trimmed

Finely chop 2 shallots. Melt 1 tablespoon butter in heavy small saucepan over medium heat. Add chopped shallots and sauté until tender, about 3 minutes. Add Madeira and green peppercorns. Boil uncovered until mixture is reduced to ⅔ cup, about 12 minutes. Remove sauce from heat.

Arrange trimmed racks of lamb on rimmed baking sheet. Cut remaining 4 shallots in half and push through garlic press. Coat lamb with pressed shallots. Sprinkle with salt and pepper. *(Can be prepared 8 hours ahead. Cover sauce and lamb separately and refrigerate.)*

Preheat oven to 400°F. Roast lamb 25 minutes. Increase heat to 500°F and continue to roast until lamb browns and meat thermometer inserted into center of lamb registers 130°F, about 5 minutes longer. Let lamb stand for 5 minutes.

Bring peppercorn sauce to simmer. Whisk in remaining 3 tablespoons butter. Season to taste with salt and pepper. Cut lamb between ribs into chops. Arrange lamb chops on plates. Spoon peppercorn sauce around lamb and serve immediately.

Warm Cinnamon-Apple Tart with Currants

Purchased puff pastry takes most of the work out of making this beautiful tart.

VARIATION: Use one large Bosc pear (peeled, cored and diced) instead of the apple.

DO-AHEAD: Bake the tart up to eight hours ahead and rewarm briefly just before serving.

2 tablespoons sugar

¾ teaspoon ground cinnamon

1 sheet frozen puff pastry (half of 17.3-ounce package), thawed

1 egg, beaten to blend (for glaze)

8 tablespoons apricot preserves

1 Golden Delicious apple (6 ounces), peeled, cored, very thinly sliced

2 tablespoons fresh lemon juice

1½ tablespoons unsalted butter

Dried currants

Vanilla ice cream

Position rack in center of oven and preheat to 400°F. Mix 2 tablespoons sugar and ½ teaspoon ground cinnamon in small bowl. Unfold thawed puff pastry on lightly floured baking sheet. Brush some of egg glaze over 1-inch border of pastry on all sides. Fold 1 inch border over to form raised edge on all sides; press edge to adhere. Using sharp knife, make ½-inch-long cuts all around pastry edge, spacing ½ inch apart. Pierce center of pastry (not edge) all over with fork. Spread 2 tablespoons apricot preserves over center of pastry. Arrange apple slices atop apricot preserves in 3 rows, overlapping apples and fitting tightly together. Brush pastry edge with some of egg glaze. Sprinkle cinnamon-sugar mixture over apples and pastry edge.

Bake tart until apples are tender and pastry is brown, about 30 minutes. Transfer tart to rack. *(Can be prepared 8 hours ahead. Rewarm in 350°F oven 8 minutes before continuing.)*

Meanwhile, mix remaining ¼ teaspoon cinnamon, 6 tablespoons apricot preserves, lemon juice and butter in small saucepan. Stir apricot sauce over medium heat until melted and hot.

Lightly dab some of apricot sauce over apples. Sprinkle with currants. Cut warm tart into 4 squares. Top each square with scoop of ice cream. Drizzle remaining sauce over ice cream.

Rosemary-roasted Salmon

Serve this with a fennel, orange and olive salad, couscous and sautéed spinach topped with toasted pine nuts. Make the Cream Cheese Pie with Peaches and Berries (see recipe) for dessert. Double the salmon recipe for a crowd.

VARIATION: A 1½- to 2-pound, two-inch-thick halibut fillet would work in this recipe.

4 SERVINGS

2 large bunches fresh rosemary

1 large red onion, thinly sliced

1 2-pound center-cut salmon fillet with skin

2 large lemons, thinly sliced

⅓ cup olive oil

Arrange half of rosemary sprigs in single layer in center of heavy baking sheet. Arrange sliced red onion atop rosemary. Place salmon, skin side down, atop red onion. Sprinkle with salt and pepper. Cover salmon with remaining rosemary sprigs. Arrange lemon slices over rosemary. Drizzle olive oil over. Sprinkle with salt. *(Can be prepared 8 hours ahead. Cover and refrigerate.)*

Preheat oven to 500°F. Roast salmon until just cooked through, about 20 minutes. Transfer salmon to plates. Serve immediately with roasted onions and lemon slices.

Cream Cheese Pie with Peaches and Berries

Blended in the processor, the no-bake cream cheese filling is ultra-smooth.

VARIATION: Top this pie with your favorite combination of seasonal fruits.

CRUST

½ cup (1 stick) unsalted butter, melted
½ teaspoon almond extract
2½ cups shortbread cookie crumbs

FILLING AND TOPPING

8 ounces cream cheese, room temperature
¾ cup powdered sugar
½ cup whipping cream
1 teaspoon vanilla extract
½ teaspoon almond extract
3 large peaches, peeled, pitted, sliced
2 ½-pint baskets fresh blackberries
¼ cup peach jam, melted

FOR CRUST: Preheat oven to 325°F. Butter 10-inch-diameter glass pie dish. Blend butter and almond extract in medium bowl. Mix in crumbs. Press over bottom and up sides of prepared dish. Bake until golden, 8 minutes. Cool.

FOR FILLING AND TOPPING: Blend cream cheese in processor until smooth. Add next 4 ingredients and blend until very smooth. Spread in crust. Chill until firm, 2 hours. Arrange peaches around edge. Arrange berries in center. Brush jam over fruit. Chill up to 3 hours.

AN ELEGANT START

Are guests coming to dinner in the middle of the week? Does a family birthday fall on a Wednesday? Your anniversary on Tuesday? With just a little bit of effort, you can begin the evening with a glass of wine and a sophisticated appetizer, an easy way to make an occasion of it. High-impact but low-effort, these ideas rely on presentation and good-quality ingredients.

- Goat Cheese Spread: Roll a log of goat cheese in lightly crushed pink peppercorns. Drizzle with extra-virgin olive oil.
- Toasted Almonds: Cook blanched shelled almonds in a mixture of oil and butter in a skillet until golden brown. Drain, cool and sprinkle with coarse salt.
- Herbed Olives: Mix Niçois or Kalamata olives with fresh rosemary, slivered garlic and dried crushed red pepper.
- Smoked Salmon: Sprinkle sliced smoked salmon with minced white onion and capers. Serve with a bowl of sour cream and toasted slices of French bread.
- Radicchio and Goat Cheese: Fill small radicchio leaves with a spoonful of goat cheese; top with crushed toasted almonds.
- Endive and Gorgonzola: Fill small Belgian endive leaves with a spoonful of Gorgonzola; top with chopped toasted walnuts.
- Prosciutto and Asparagus: Wrap thin slices of prosciutto around steamed asparagus spears (this works with breadsticks, too).

Rib Roast with Thyme-Mustard Jus

Serve with sautéed teardrop tomatoes and mashed sweet potatoes. The Pear Spice Cake with Pecan Praline Topping (see recipe) completes the meal.

VARIATION: For extra flavor, whisk one cup sour cream with two tablespoons prepared horse-radish to serve with this gorgeous roast.

6 SERVINGS

½ cup honey-Dijon mustard

3 teaspoons chopped fresh thyme

1 3½- to 4-pound boneless prime rib beef roast, excess fat trimmed

½ cup water

¼ cup dry white wine

Mix mustard and 2 teaspoons thyme in small bowl. Place beef in heavy large roasting pan. Coat beef with mustard mixture. Cover; let stand 1½ hours at room temperature or refrigerate overnight.

Preheat oven to 375°F. Scrape off marinade from beef; reserve marinade. Roast beef 1 hour. Brush reserved marinade over beef. Roast until thermometer inserted into center of beef registers 120°F, about 10 minutes longer. Transfer beef to cutting board. Tent with foil to keep warm.

Pour pan juices into 1-cup glass measuring cup. Spoon fat off top of pan juices. Return juices to pan. Place pan atop burners on medium-high heat. Add ½ cup water and wine. Boil until juices are reduced to ½ cup, scraping up any browned bits. Stir in remaining 1 teaspoon thyme.

Cut beef into ½-inch-thick slices. Sprinkle with salt and pepper. Serve beef with reduced juices.

Pear Cake with Pecan Praline Topping

Fresh pears, crystallized ginger and nuts really perk up this boxed spice cake.

DO-AHEAD: Note that this can be prepared a day ahead. The topping will be soft when served warm; it will be firmer, like southern praline, when cool.

---

1 cup (2 sticks) unsalted butter

1 box spice cake mix (1 pound 2.25 ounces)

¾ cup canned pear nectar

3 large eggs

2 tablespoons mild-flavored (light) molasses

½ cup minced crystallized ginger

2 pears, peeled, cored, cut into ½-inch pieces (about 1½ cups)

¾ cup (packed) golden brown sugar

¼ cup whipping cream

1⅓ cups pecan halves, toasted

Position rack in center of oven and preheat to 350°F. Butter 9-inch-diameter springform pan with 2¾-inch-high sides. Stir ½ cup butter in small saucepan over medium heat until melted and brown, about 3 minutes. Pour into large bowl. Add spice cake mix, canned pear nectar, eggs, molasses and crystallized ginger. Using electric mixer, beat batter 2 minutes. Fold in chopped pears. Pour batter into prepared springform pan. Bake until cake is dark brown and tester inserted into center comes out with some moist crumbs attached, about 1 hour 10 minutes.

Cool cake in pan on rack 15 minutes. Run small sharp knife between pan sides and cake to loosen. Release pan sides. Place cake on platter.

Stir brown sugar, whipping cream and remaining ½ cup butter in heavy medium saucepan over medium-high heat until smooth. Boil 3 minutes, stirring often. Stir in pecan halves. Spoon warm topping over warm cake. Serve warm or at room temperature. *(Can be prepared 1 day ahead. Cover with cake dome and store at room temperature.)*

Index

Page numbers in *italics* indicate color photographs.

Acknowledgments

In memory of Bill Garry, mentor and friend, who championed this book in its early days. *Laurie Buckle*

The editor would like to thank the following people for their assistance and support in producing this book: Karen Kaplan and Kristine Kidd, for their many recipes, past and present; Sandra Frank, for nutritional information; Andrea Lucich, food stylist; and Carol Hacker/Tableprop, prop stylist.

The following people contributed the recipes included in this book:

Allgood's Bar and Grill,
Big Sky, Montana
Melanie Barnard
Ed Behr
Bonnie Bennett
John H. Bialas
Laurie Black
Elizabeth L. Brown
Meg and Paul Brown
Cattleman's Steakhouse,
Oklahoma City, Oklahoma
Patricia Connell
Kathi Dameron
Brooke Dojny
Jeanne Fadely
Jim Fobel
Rozanne Gold

Aviva Goldfarb
Kathy Grady
Nancy Grubin
Ken Haedrich
Ginny Hamisch
Judy Harmon
Lai Ching Heen,
Kowloon, Hong Kong
Jessica Hirschman
Karen Kaplan
Jeanne Thiel Kelley
Kristine Kidd
Elinor Klivans
Dona Kuryanowicz
Bob Lawrence
The Lord Jeffery Inn,
Amherst, Massachusetts

Brenda Louch
Peggy Markel
Marie T. Mora
Jinx and Jefferson Morgan
Rochelle Palermo
Christine Piccin
Rick Rodgers
Betty Rosbottom
Richard Sax
Marie Simmons
Sarah Tenaglia
Beth and Tom Tiernan
Charlie Trotter
Mary Vaughan
Todd Weisz,
Turnberry Isle Resort & Club,
Aventura, Florida